Glorious One-Pot Meals

Glorious
ONE-POT
Meals

A Revolutionary
New Quick and Healthy Approach
to Dutch-Oven Cooking

ELIZABETH YARNELL

Clarkson Potter/Publishers
New York

Published in the United States by Clarkson Potter/Publishers, an imprint of
the Crown Publishing Group, a division of Random House, Inc., New York.
www.crownpublishing.com
www.clarksonpotter.com

Clarkson N. Potter is a trademark and Potter and colophon
are registered trademarks of Random House, Inc.

A previous edition of this work was published in the United States by
Pomegranate Consulting, LLC, Denver, Colorado, in 2005, and a revised
edition of this work was subsequently published in the United States by
Broadway Books, an imprint of the Crown Publishing Group, a division of
Random House, Inc. New York in 2009.

Book design by Elizabeth Rendfleisch

Library of Congress Cataloging-in-Publication Data
Yarnell, Elizabeth.
Glorious one-pot meals : a revolutionary new quick and healthy approach
to Dutch-oven cooking/Elizabeth Yarnell.
p.   cm.
Previously published: Denver, Colo. : Pomegranate Consulting, 2005.
Includes index.
1. Dutch oven cookery. 2. One-dish meals. 3. Quick and easy cookery.
I. Title.

TX840.D88Y37 2009
641.5'89—dc22
2008023029

ISBN 978-0-7679-3010-9

PRINTED IN THE UNITED STATES OF AMERICA

11

Revised Edition

This book is dedicated to my husband,
Edward Cope, who not only cocreated the Glorious One-Pot Meal
cooking method with me but also ate every meal set before him
with gusto and compliments. And to the many fans around the world who have been
enjoying their Glorious One-Pot Meals and telling their friends about them.
May you all eat well and be healthy.

CONTENTS

FOREWORD

Elizabeth Yarnell has developed a remarkably simple method of putting a delicious, healthy dinner on the table quickly and easily. Her own quest for fast, fresh, nutritious meals led her to create this revolutionary one-pot preparation system.

She first introduced me to the unique one-pot meals by preparing a sampling of her recipes. I was amazed and impressed by these delectable dinners that took no time at all to prepare. As a health-conscious cook, I am delighted that the recipes can be made with very little fat and with a variety of fresh vegetables and lean meats. The results are flavorful, nutritious meals for the entire family to enjoy.

I added Elizabeth's Glorious One-Pot Meals to the class schedule at The Seasoned Chef Cooking School and was astounded by the popularity of her classes. The concept of this unique cooking method caught on right away and her classes filled up immediately. Classes were added to accommodate lengthy waiting lists of students eager to simplify their dinner preparation.

We've seen everyone from restaurant owners to teenagers, from stay-at-home moms to empty-nesters take her classes. In the seven years that Elizabeth has taught Glorious One-Pot Meals at The Seasoned Chef, many students have returned every time she has offered a class. They're always hungry for her newest recipes. I know that they—and many others—will be delighted that she has published this marvelous cookbook with a variety of delectable recipes!

I like to introduce Elizabeth's classes by saying that this is a cooking method where, once you have the meal prepared and in the oven, you can sit down and relax (perhaps with a glass of wine!), knowing your Glorious One Pot Meal doesn't need any more attention until it is ready for the table.

Our cooking school students—home chefs with busy work and family schedules—appreciate the ease and convenience of preparing dinner with just one pot to clean up. They have enjoyed success with Elizabeth's one-pot meals; I know you will too.

Susan Stevens, M.A., R.D.
Director
The Seasoned Chef Cooking School
Denver, Colorado
www.TheSeasonedChef.com

ACKNOWLEDGMENTS

This cookbook is a credit to a true grass-roots effort.

John and Jesse Cahill gave my husband and me our first enameled cast-iron Dutch oven as a wedding gift. Our thought then was, "Oh, how cute. How do we use it?" Good friend Corinne Snyder commented to me that we ate really well and asked me to teach her how to cook like we did, sparking the first draft of *Glorious One-Pot Meals*. My in-laws, including Judy and Tony Cope, Peter and Leslie Cope, John and Stephanie Donohue, and Andrew and Lisa Cope, became de facto recipe testers. My aunt, Jane Cotler, was my tireless cheerleader, recipe tester, and draft editor. My cousin Emily Cotler builds all of my gorgeous Web sites, designed the logo, and has always dropped everything else to help me make this happen. My cousin Abi Bowling is my Web guru and valuable tech support service, and cousin Julie Pottinger my role model for succeeding as an author.

My wonderful MS support group based in southeast Denver and headed by Connie Harris became early recipe testers. Jennifer Gennaro told me she believed that I got MS in order to invent this new cooking method and help the world eat better. My Bodyshops Toastmasters group cheered me on and gave me the confidence and skills to speak in public. Rocky Mountain PBS invited me to demonstrate a recipe in their 2001 Cookathon, and then reran it numerous times, giving me my first television exposure.

Sally Stich, the best writing teacher I will ever have, Leslie Petrovski, and Lara Riscol all edited my early manuscript and book proposal as I set out to find an agent and a publisher. Susan Stevens of The Seasoned Chef Cooking School not only allowed me to teach but also gave me targeted feedback on both my recipe writing and my teaching style. My patent attorney, Henry L. Smith, Jr., took my five pages of gibberish and turned it into a twenty-five-page patent (U.S. no. 6,846,504, Canada no. 2,401,092), making me a bona fide inventor.

If it weren't for the vision of my agent, Stacey Glick, and my talented editor, Jennifer Josephy, you wouldn't be holding this edition in your hands today.

My mother, Susan Rutherford, and stepfather, Phil Stietenroth, tested numerous recipes, took my professional photographs and early videos, loaned me money to get my business going, and believed in me even when I didn't. My father and stepmother, Phil and Barbara Yarnell, helped to fund my first print run, contributed recipes, and encouraged me to pursue my dreams. My sister Molly Skyar urged me to grab for the brass ring even when I thought it was futile. My sister Katie Yarnell provided babysitting that allowed me to make this book happen, and my brother, Jared Yarnell, dared me to succeed.

Finally, I acknowledge my beautiful children, Jeremy and Lilia Cope, who through their very existence encourage me to seek a healthy lifestyle. And last but not least, I thank my husband, Edward Cope, whose support has never waivered. Without my partner, my best friend, my lover, my soul mate, none of this would have happened. I am very lucky indeed.

Glorious One-Pot Meals

INTRODUCTION

Strange to see how a good dinner and feasting reconciles everybody.

Samuel Pepys

Imagine coming home after a long day, reaching into your refrigerator, freezer, and pantry, and—in five to twenty minutes—tossing enough food for an entire meal into a single pot and walking away from the kitchen. A half hour to forty-five minutes later you serve up a scrumptious meal of chicken bathed in a peanut-satay sauce served on rice with a variety of crisp-tender vegetables. Or perhaps succulent scallops tinged with ginger on a bed of chunky sweet potatoes, with an array of mushrooms and broccoli to round out the meal. Sound like a dream?

Our daily lives often seem to run on overdrive, and too frequently a home-cooked, healthy dinner is one of the sacrifices made. We're too busy to cook properly, we complain. Or perhaps we just don't know how to cook healthfully, or aren't even sure we can identify healthy foods beyond lettuce. Surely we all want to feed ourselves and our families nutritious meals so we will live long and healthy lives, but until now there haven't been many solutions for getting a good, nutritious meal on the table quickly.

It seems that while most people would prefer to eat home-cooked meals, in reality they don't more often than they do. In fact, 82 percent of Americans say they enjoy preparing food at home and more than half claim they would cook at home more often if it didn't take so much time. Further, while 65 percent of us say we are trying to eat healthier foods, one-third report not having the time to prepare healthy meals. Part of the problem may be the lack of a good way to cook that meets all our needs for speed, convenience, ease, and nutrition.

This was certainly the problem I faced as a newlywed and business owner diagnosed with a debilitating disease. I wanted to improve my diet and the course of my disease, but I lacked the time and stamina for long, complicated meal-preparation marathons. I wished there were an easier way to cook healthier foods. So I began experimenting and soon discovered a new and different way of cooking that met my needs: I call it *infusion cooking.*

Infusion cooking refers to using a lidded cast-iron Dutch oven to hold layers of whole foods and flash-cooking them inside a superhot oven for a brief time. No added liquid means that these recipes are not stews but rather complete meals where each item retains its cellular integrity and emerges perfectly intact. The intense heat causes the vegetables to release their moisture, which presses up against the food and infuses it with clean flavors from herbs, spices, and other natural ingredients.

Vegetables stay crisp. Meats are moist. Grains fluff nicely. It's as if you used three or four pots and pans to create a complete and balanced dinner, only you didn't have to juggle the timing of different dishes or hover over a hot stove or face a daunting clean-up task. Pretty cool. That's why I call these recipes Glorious One-Pot Meals: They allow me to serve deliciously healthy dinners with very little effort—a *glorious* feeling!

Make no mistake: These are not recipes for your slow cooker. You will not find casseroles, skillet meals, stir-fries, or even simmered stews in this cookbook.

Instead, *Glorious One-Pot Meals* offers a revolutionary new way to think about planning, shopping for, preparing, cooking, and eating dinner. This method is so different that it has been awarded both U.S. (no. 6,846,504) and Canadian (no. 2,401,092) patents. So far, I haven't discovered any previously published recipes that use this particular cooking technique. I guarantee that you will be amazed at how easy it can be to put together mouthwatering meals in less than half an hour.

First, follow a few recipes to discover how truly easy and delicious Glorious One-Pot Meals can be. Be bold about substituting ingredients as advised. Then take the plunge and become an intuitive cook by creating your own meals out of your favorite foods. Appreciated for its convenience and simplicity, the infusion cooking technique demystifies cooking for those who fear the kitchen, while still offering the textural complexity and depth of flavors demanded by more accomplished chefs.

It has been said that there are only nine cooking methods on this planet: sauté, fry, bake, broil, grill, slow-cook, braise, boil, and steam. With infusion cooking, there are now ten. Soon, a cast-iron Dutch oven will be as prevalent as a slow cooker in the battery of utensils available to the home cook.

My focus had been in finding a solution to my problem, not in inventing a new way to cook. However, what resulted may be viewed as the missing link between eating conveniently and eating healthfully. Happy cooking and eating!

WHAT YOU NEED TO KNOW

*Part of the secret of success in life is to eat what you like
and let the food fight it out inside.*

Mark Twain

WHAT IS A GLORIOUS ONE-POT MEAL?

Glorious One-Pot Meals call for whole foods rather than processed and packaged items, and you'll find that each recipe—even the vegetarian ones—offers a complete and balanced meal of an appropriate amount of protein, a variety of vegetables, and a healthy serving of carbohydrates.

While many other familiar one-pot meals require a side dish of pasta or rice made separately, or even a salad or bread, Glorious One-Pot Meal recipes are intended to provide the entire meal *in just one pot*—nothing else is needed, not even a salad. Each meal is complete in and of itself and offers a range of nutritional benefits.

The centerpiece of the infusion cooking technique is the Dutch oven. If you haven't used a Dutch oven since you were a Scout, relax: It has grown up. Today's Dutch oven is not the heavy, blackened behemoth that simmered baked beans for fifty at the cookout all those years ago. Lighter in weight

than those of old, sometimes coated with a nonstick surface of fired-on enamel, and often dishwasher-safe, modern Dutch ovens still carry a core of cast iron but now come in a wide variety of brands, sizes, shapes, and colors.

Any shape or brand of cast-iron Dutch oven works well with this technique: Round or oval ovens are most common, but you might also see snowflakes, hearts, eggplants, apples, and other fanciful shapes. As a result of its unique heat-conduction properties, cast iron works best for this cooking method; you won't experience the same guaranteed results using a pot made of another material.

Personally, I prefer enamel-coated cast iron over uncoated cast iron for a variety of reasons: (1) Enamel-coated Dutch ovens are lighter, an important consideration since you will be loading the pot with food and then lifting it in and out of a hot oven; (2) enamel-coated cast iron doesn't need seasoning and won't rust; and (3) most enamel-coated cast-iron Dutch ovens are dishwasher-safe, making clean-up even more of a breeze. However, uncoated cast-iron Dutch ovens perform just as well when cooking Glorious One-Pot Meals, and may be less expensive.

Some readers have had limited success using stainless-steel Dutch ovens as long as they have the essential characteristics of a Dutch oven: a wide, flat bottom, vertical (not sloped) sides, and a lid with a ridge on the underside that sits heavily and securely on the pot.

The recipes in this book are based on using a two-quart Dutch oven to provide a complete dinner for two adult eaters. If you're cooking for more than two, you will want to double or triple the recipes and use a larger Dutch oven (see the Recipe Adjustment Chart, page 12).

HOW DOES IT WORK?

One cannot think well, love well, sleep well, if one has not dined well.
Virginia Woolf

As mentioned earlier, Glorious One-Pot Meals work by infusion cooking—the process in which ingredients are placed in a covered Dutch oven and heated rapidly in a hot oven, releasing the moisture from the vegetables and trapping the steam inside the pot, which in turn cooks the food and infuses it with flavor. Because the hot steam is trapped against the food instead of evaporating, it cooks the food quickly and retains moisture. The method is deceptively simple, yet it produces complex flavors and aromas and enhances ordinarily mild flavors while retaining much of the nutritional value of the food.

The critical elements that ensure successful Glorious One-Pot Meals are (1) using a cast-iron Dutch oven, (2) baking in a 450°F (Fahrenheit) oven, and (3) layering the ingredients in a specific order.

Since an oven ten degrees off in either direction will negatively affect a Glorious One-Pot Meal, it's worthwhile to verify the temperature with an oven thermometer.

Resist the urge to lift the lid of the pot too early—you don't want to release the steam that's infusing the food with flavor. Go sit down, relax! You'll know your meal is ready when you can smell the aroma escaping from the oven. This is your *three-minute warning:* Give your meal another three minutes of baking and then pull out the pot, lift the lid, and serve immediately. No more fussing at the stovetop while everyone else is already eating, no preparing rice or pasta separately, no need to make a salad; just bring the Dutch oven to the table and serve.

The infusion cooking method eliminates the obstacles that prevent us from cooking healthier, more nutritious meals by making it almost effortless to put dinner together and by significantly reducing the after-dinner cleanup chore. Choose a simple recipe for those days when you just need to get food on the table fast, and save more complex recipes for when you can spare the energy for a little more effort.

A typical Glorious One-Pot Meal for two people requires less than twenty minutes to prepare and thirty to forty-five minutes to bake. Build your pot at an earlier, more convenient moment, keep it refrigerated, and then move it directly into a fully preheated oven a half hour or so before dinnertime.

Forget menu planning and detailed recipes. Instead, use a very basic shopping list of staples to stock your kitchen: meat, fish, or poultry (fresh or frozen); in-season vegetables in as many colors as possible; pasta, rice, or another grain; and a few fresh herbs. (See the sample shopping list on page 23.) To increase the variety in each meal, use just part of a vegetable and seal the rest in the fridge for a future meal. There's no need to thaw anything from the freezer because Glorious One-Pot Meals accept any mix of fresh, frozen, and canned foods, usually with minimal or no adjustment of oven time.

Glorious One-Pot Meals work with anything from simple chopped fresh herbs to complex spice medleys or flavorful marinades. Use your favorite vinaigrette salad dressing as a marinade; add jarred condiments such as salsa, teriyaki sauce, and mustard; or just count on the pure flavors of salt, pepper, and garlic to enhance your creation. Almost any familiar flavor combination or exotic culinary culture can be interpreted as a Glorious One-Pot Meal with a little bit of creativity and intuition.

Go easy on yourself and try a few of the suggestions here that contain ingredients you already know you like. Or add things you do like to the recommended recipe.

Don't like meat? Hate onions? Leave them out. Don't want to eat protein and carbs together? Then don't add them to the same meal. Glorious One-Pot Meal cooking is an adventure you know will always turn out well because you choose the ingredients and flavors you like each and every time.

nation of ingredients. If you're not adding a certain type of ingredient, such as pasta or meat, simply skip that step and continue with the process. I encourage you to fill the pot to the brim with veggies to take advantage of the extra space available when something else is omitted from a recipe.

The Infused Cooking Technique

There is no sincerer love than the love of food.
George Bernard Shaw

The main premise for constructing a Glorious One-Pot Meal is to layer. While building a lasagna means interspersing sheets of pasta with meat, cheese, and tomato sauce, building a Glorious One-Pot Meal means layering the ingredients across the bottom of the pot in order of *type:* dry goods, protein, root vegetables, above-ground vegetables, and herbs, spices, and other flavorings. Don't be afraid to freely mix and match fresh and frozen items as they will all emerge perfectly cooked at the end!

This basic technique for making infused one-pot meals is adaptable for any combi-

Common Measurements for Successful Glorious One-Pot Meals

The portions in the Glorious One-Pot Meal recipes presented in this cookbook feed two people and use a two-quart cast-iron Dutch oven. Adjust the measurements (see pages 8 to 9) and size of oven accordingly to feed more people.

Basic Tips for Glorious One-Pot Meal Success

THE RECIPES AND TECHNIQUE

Consider the recipes in this book as guidelines rather than gospel. Feel free to substitute or omit an ingredient or change a

COMMON MEASUREMENTS

Ingredient	Liquid	Notes
$^1/_2$ to $^3/_4$ pound meat		Try to use boneless cuts of meat, especially if frozen when added to the pot.
2 to 4 pieces or $^1/_2$ to $^3/_4$ pound poultry		Consider a leg-thigh unit a single piece even though you may have to separate the parts to fit them in the Dutch oven.
$^1/_2$ to $^3/_4$ pound fish		Fish can be fillets, steaks, or whole minus the head. Be aware that frozen steaks containing large bones may take longer to cook.
1 cup pasta	$^1/_3$ cup	Add 3 to 4 drops of olive oil to the water to keep the pasta from sticking together. For a meal based on pasta, double these measurements. Pasta shapes that give the best results: orzo, penne, rotini, farfalle, macaroni, and other short, chunky shapes.
1 cup white rice	1 cup + 1 tablespoon	For the most consistent results, rinse rice in a strainer under cold water until the water runs clear before adding to the pot. If the rice is still crunchy when the meal is done, fluff with a fork and then put the lid back on and let the pot sit for an additional few minutes to fully hydrate.
1 cup brown rice	1 cup	Use instant brown rice that has been parboiled and precooked for best results. Or try soaking raw, rinsed long-grain brown rice in $1^1/_4$ cups boiling water in the covered Dutch oven for about 15 minutes. Strain and return rice to pot with final $1^1/_4$ cups boiling broth or water before adding other ingredients (the rice may also require extra cooking time).
$^1/_2$ cup couscous	$^1/_2$ cup + 1 tablespoon	Whole wheat couscous works just as well as the non-whole-grain version. Some grains may emerge toasted and crunchy; be sure to stir well to coat each grain with liquid, and fluff with a fork when serving.

Ingredient	Liquid	Notes
3/4 cup quinoa	1 cup	See preceding couscous notes about toasted grains.
1/2 cup polenta	1 1/2 cups	Use dry polenta, not prehydrated. Grits can be substituted.
1/4 cup barley	1/2 cup	Hulled barley is a whole grain while pearled barley has been further refined. Either can be used here.
1 cup bulgur	1/2 cup	Bulgur is a form of wheat where the wheat berries are steamed, dried, and can be ground fine or coarse.
3/4 cup amaranth	3/4 cup	Amaranth is an ancient whole grain that looks a bit like tapioca.
1/2 cup kasha	1 cup	Kasha refers to toasted buckwheat groats.
1/2 cup lentils	3/4 cup	Lentils cooked this way emerge firm and defined; if you prefer softer lentils, substitute drained canned lentils and omit the liquid called for to hydrate the dry lentils.
1 tablespoon fresh herbs		This measurement applies to each fresh herb you include. For rosemary and thyme, use 3 to 6 intact sprigs and remove before serving.
1/2 to 1 teaspoon dry spices		Again, this measurement applies to each dry spice you include, whether used in a mixture or just sprinkled into the pot.
1/4 cup marinade		A good marinade has both acidic (as in vinegar, lemon juice, wine) and alkaline (as in olive, vegetable, or peanut oil) elements. Avoid cream-based dressings.

recipe in almost any sense to produce the delicious dinner you and your family *want* to eat. With some practice and confidence you can become an intuitive cook with *Glorious One-Pot Meals*.

Start by following a few recipes closely before branching out to create your own. This will help you to get the feel for the pot and the cooking method and enable you to apply the layering precepts to other ingredients. Remember that the key is the layering. The more recipes you prepare, the more you'll understand which ingredients to use, how they should be cut, and in what order they should be added to your Dutch oven.

The *only* elements in a Glorious One-Pot Meal recipe that require exact measurements are the ratios between dry grains and the liquid needed to hydrate them. Be sure to use the appropriate measuring cups for dry and wet ingredients. (See "Common Measurements," pages 8 and 9.)

Adding more liquid produces a poached effect, which is delicious but not always desired. The correct proportion of liquid to ingredients keeps the cooking process inside the food, infusing it with flavors throughout the pot. (Refer to the "Common Measurements" chart, pages 8 and 9, when in doubt as to grain-to-liquid ratios.)

To stretch a meal to feed more people, prepare grains or pasta separately in a traditional manner and fill the Dutch oven to the brim with more vegetables and/or meat.

THE OVEN

Preheat your oven to 450°F as you prepare the ingredients (450°F is equivalent to 230°C or Mark 8 in Europe). By the time your Glorious One-Pot Meal is ready to bake, the oven will be hot.

Use a stand-alone oven thermometer to validate the oven temperature, as temperatures off by even ten degrees will affect the results of your meal.

Place the rack in the center of the oven. Don't allow the knob on the lid of the Dutch oven to touch the heating element on the ceiling of the oven.

There is no benefit to using a convection oven as a convection oven speeds cooking of *uncovered* foods and Glorious One-Pot Meals *remain covered* the entire time they bake. Plus, cooking time and temperature are the same for a conventional oven as for a convection oven for these meals, so you may as well save energy by using a conventional oven if you have the choice.

THE INGREDIENTS

The infusion cooking process clearly enhances the original characteristics of a meat or vegetable, so start with good-quality ingredients.

Use a sturdy vegetable scrubber and clean vegetables well. No peeling is necessary, but it's important that all produce is clean and that bruises, eyes, and other blemishes are removed. Even if you're using organic vegetables, it's still a good idea to use a fruit and vegetable wash of citrus and baking soda to remove any residue of wax or grime. For conventionally grown vegetables, a wash is essential to remove the coating of chemicals.

Rinse pieces of meat and poultry and trim off the fat. Fat won't melt off a piece of meat or poultry in the Dutch oven the way it can when grilling or frying. Removing the skin from poultry makes for a lower-fat meal.

Keep some frozen vegetables around to add on a whim to any Glorious One-Pot Meal; no need to defrost. Canned tomatoes and jars of prepared tomato sauce are also recommended staples. See "The Stocked Pantry" (page 18) for more ideas on what to keep around.

Wrap and freeze cleaned and trimmed meat, poultry, and fish in individual servings. It's always easier to reach into the freezer than to run to the grocery store at dinnertime, and individual serving sizes allow you to customize the meal. Also, meat will cook better if the pieces are not frozen together.

Whole, peeled garlic cloves add a light garlicky flavor to meat while mellowing into a tasty, nutty treat. The more garlic is cut and the cellular walls are injured, the more intense the flavor. Adjust garlic intensity by mincing, chopping, slicing, or by simply leaving the peeled cloves intact. You may find you use more garlic with infusion cooking than you do in other cooking methods.

Instant brown rice has been parboiled,

precooked, and then dried and packaged. It looks just like regular rice, except it is a whole grain rather than a refined one, with nothing artificial added. Substitute equally for white rice in any recipe. Fluff all grains with a fork when serving.

At times you might run out of room and still have cut vegetables left over. Seal and refrigerate extra pieces for use in the next Glorious One-Pot Meal, or chop vegetables into smaller pieces and repack the pot. My husband insists that sometimes the key is in the packing; changing the size or organization of the ingredients can affect how compactly the pot is packed. We try to pack our Dutch oven to the brim with vegetables every time.

To improve the nutritional profile of a recipe, use low-sodium options for ingredients such as broth and canned tomatoes, as well as for seasonings such as soy sauce. Consider choosing no-sugar-added ketchup and peanut butter as well.

GLORIOUS ONE-POT MEALS AND DUTCH OVENS

Each recipe in *Glorious One-Pot Meals* is intended to be prepared in a 2-quart Dutch oven and will feed two people, with possibly a little left over, depending upon the enthusiasm of the diners. Once you increase the size of the Dutch oven, follow the one-quart-per-person rule minus a half-quart. So, for dinner for four, I find the $3^1/2$-quart pot holds plenty of food. See the table below to determine the right pot for your needs.

RECIPE ADJUSTMENT CHART

Diners	Dutch oven size (quarts)	Recipe adjustment	Approximate baking time
2	2	none	45 minutes
4	$3^1/2$–4	+/- double	53 minutes
6	$5^1/2$–6	+/- triple	60 minutes

Dutch-oven manufacturers often offer either whole-quart or half-quart sizes. When considering a half-quart size, I assume it will hold enough food if I decrease the one-quart-per-person rule by a half-quart.

Certainly it is fine to cook a smaller amount, say for two people, in a larger Dutch oven, say a 5-quart size. Just be aware that the amount of time needed to cook may or may not change (use your nose to know for sure when dinner is ready). Some recipes may dry out a little, and you may fall victim to what I like to call "overenthusiastic vegetable preparation." Overenthusiastic vegetable preparation means that, because your pot is so large, it is hard to know when you've put in enough food, and it's easy to overdo the proportion of vegetables to meat and carbs. All this means is that if you use a pot size larger than needed, follow your nose rather than a timer and be prepared to have a lot of veggie leftovers.

Buy the size of Dutch oven appropriate for the number of people you feed on a daily basis. It's just easier to use the right size pot. After that, if you decide to make Glorious One-Pot Meals when you entertain guests, you may want to get a second, larger pot. By this point, you won't have any doubt as to how valuable this piece of cookware is because you will have experienced the amazing benefits of infusion cooking.

CARING FOR YOUR DUTCH OVEN

Cast-iron Dutch ovens are an investment and require special care. When using uncoated cast-iron pots, follow the rules of caring for all uncoated cast-iron cookware:

1. Season before use by bonding a thin layer of grease onto the cooking surface. To season a new pot, heat the oven to 250°–300°F. Coat the pot with lard and place it in the oven for fifteen minutes. Remove the pot and pour out any excess grease. Put it back in the oven and bake for about two hours.
2. Rinse the pot with hot water to clean it; *never* use soap.
3. Dry the pot completely and store coated with a thin layer of cooking oil to prevent rust.

While some enamel-coated cast-iron Dutch ovens can go directly from freezer to oven to table to dishwasher with no problem, there are a few guidelines to follow in caring for these as well:

1. Use wooden or plastic utensils. Metal utensils can scratch the enamel coating.
2. Cool a cast-iron Dutch oven before immersing it in water. Hot cast iron can crack when it comes into contact with water or something very cold. It should be cool to the touch before washing.
3. Clean enamel-coated cast iron with a soft sponge and liquid dish detergent. Abrasive cleaners or steel wool pads can seriously damage the pot. Fill the pot with hot soapy water and let sit for fifteen minutes or so before cleaning for best results.

Many enamel-coated cast-iron Dutch ovens are not intended to go into a 450°F oven because of the plastic knob on the lid. But over the decade that I have been using my collection of ovens for this technique and preparing hundreds, if not thousands, of Glorious One-Pot Meals, my knobs have remained pristine. Of the tens of thousands of early adapters of this cooking method, only one has ever reported a faulty knob (the company replaced it). And I have been assured by one major manufacturer that the intention was to deter cooks from using a superhot oven for a long period of time, significantly longer than one hour.

ESSENTIAL EQUIPMENT

The fundamental tools for creating Glorious One-Pot Meals include the following kitchen basics:

CAST-IRON DUTCH OVEN, preferably enamel-coated cast iron. (See "Recipe Adjustment Chart," page 12, to determine the appropriate size for you.)

PLASTIC OR WOODEN SERVING SPOON. Avoid metal utensils as they may scratch the enamel coating or seasoning of the Dutch oven.

SHARP KNIFE. A dull knife can double the labor of chopping vegetables and increase the risk of injury because of the extra force needed to cut. A happy chef has a good-quality knife.

PLASTIC CUTTING BOARD. Meat, poultry, and fish should never be placed on a wooden cutting board because wood can trap bacteria. Plastic cutting boards can be washed clean and are dishwasher-safe for added health security.

PLASTIC OR WOODEN CUTTING BOARD. Keep your vegetable cutting board free from contact with meat.

RUBBER SCRUBBIE SPONGE. Avoid steel wool or other abrasive cleaners on an enamel-coated Dutch oven. I find a "safe for all surfaces" sponge with a gentle plastic mesh on one side is perfect for many uses.

VEGETABLE SCRUBBER. A soft vegetable brush helps remove dirt from tubers and other root vegetables and can eliminate the need to peel the item before cooking it.

MESH STRAINER. Useful for rinsing everything from fresh herbs and string beans to dry rice. Be sure the strainer is fine enough that rice grains won't slip through the weave.

TWO POT HOLDERS. A heavy Dutch oven plus a very hot oven can be a recipe for burns, so always take care when moving the pot. Don't forget that the knob on the lid will also be 450°F. Take precautions not to burn yourself.

TRIVET. For obvious reasons, don't set a hot Dutch oven directly on a surface that isn't heat-resistant.

COLOR YOUR MEAL NUTRITIOUS: THE VEGETABLE STORY

When designing Glorious One-Pot Meals, I consider many factors: type and intensity of flavors, authenticity of the ingredients to the specific culinary tradition, and the nutritional benefits of all the components. Since each color family of vegetables offers different nutritional benefits, I aim to include several colors of veggies in each recipe.

If you think of the meal as a canvas and bring color into the pot by including a variety of green, yellow, red, and orange vegetables, not only will your taste buds be stimulated, but your body will receive a broad selection of vitamins, minerals, and nutrients every time you dine.

The chart on page 16 gives a quick glance at what color means in a vegetable.

Experiment and have fun with your food. Push aside the iceberg lettuce (almost devoid of nutrients) and use sweet potatoes, leeks, broccoli, asparagus, eggplant— whatever is in season or strikes your fancy. Glorious One-Pot Meals are designed to be complete dinners; there's no need to serve a side salad because multiple vegetables are

COLOR YOUR MEAL NUTRITIOUS

Color	Vegetables	Nutrients	Benefits
Orange/Yellow	Carrots, winter squash, sweet potatoes	Beta-carotene	• Maintain healthy vision • Enhance immunity • Encourage healthy skin • Prevent cancer
		Potassium	• Enable muscle contraction • Maintain healthy blood pressure
	Corn, potatoes	Vitamin A	• Promote healthy eyesight • Prevent night blindness • Build resistance to respiratory infections
Green	Broccoli, kale and other leafy greens, soybeans, legumes, cabbage		
		Calcium	• Promote bone health
	Algae	Iron	• Enrich blood
	Brussels sprouts, peas, spinach, romaine lettuce	Folate	• Prevent birth defects • Prevent heart disease • Promote healthy red blood cells
		Vitamin C	• Strengthen immunity • Function as an antioxidant
Red	Tomatoes, eggplant, beets, garlic, leeks, onions	Phytochemicals	• Function as antioxidants • Prevent cancer
Brown	Mushrooms	Riboflavin (vitamin B_{12})	• Produce energy in cells

included in every meal. And don't forget that variety is essential to receive the broadest range of nutrients your body needs.

Beware of overly ambitious vegetable preparation—a Dutch oven can hold only so much. Including entire vegetables in a two-quart pot may work against maximum color variation goals. Instead, consider using just half or one-third of a vegetable such as a green pepper. Store the rest in the fridge—or cut it up and freeze it—for your next meal.

Veggies You Always Loved to Hate

Limp asparagus, bitter Brussels sprouts dripping with fat, and sticky-sweet candied yams are some of the vegetables Americans love to hate. Overcooking or overprocessing vegetables breaks down their flavor, texture, and nutritional benefits.

The beauty of infusion cooking is that vegetables emerge from the oven firm yet tender and perfectly cooked every time. Add vegetables with abandon. Toss in zucchini, carrots, potatoes, even turnips, spinach, and tomatoes—all at the same time. When the aroma of a finished meal wafts from your oven, all will be cooked perfectly.

Do you have painful childhood memories of swallowing beets whole to clear your plate? Beets in a Glorious One-Pot Meal are heavenly; they add extra heartiness and vibrant color to any recipe. No need to peel; just scrub them well and trim the ends. Then cut into one-inch cubes or strips and place close to the bottom of the pot (in the root vegetable layer). You'll savor every mouthful.

Turnips, too, have a terrible reputation for bitterness. But in a Glorious One-Pot Meal, tender morsels infused with a mild, almost sweet, flavor emerge from the pot. Peeling is optional. Wash and trim the ends, then cut into small chunks, no larger than $3/4$ inch. Turnips also go in the root vegetable layer.

Oh, for an ode to the Brussels sprout. It forms a perfect miniature cabbage in imitation of its much larger cousins. I often crave the shot of iron from its jade leaves, so sweet and firm when cooked this way. You may surprise yourself and become a Brussels sprout convert once you try them prepared this way.

Spinach is a versatile ingredient that can add green to almost any infused one-pot meal recipe. The secret to enjoying spinach or its cousin, kale, is to be certain all the grit has been removed. Nothing ruins a good bite of spinach like biting down on sand. A simple spinach-washing technique is to drop the separated leaves into a large, wide-mouthed bowl and fill with cold water. Swish things around for a bit and then let settle for a few minutes. All of the dirt will sift to the bottom of the bowl. Lift the leaves from the bowl and gently shake to remove large drops. Trim the stems at the base and tear off any overmature spots.

Get ready. You're going to love your vegetables in a Glorious One-Pot Meal.

THE STOCKED PANTRY: HEALTHY CONVENIENCE FOODS

A main benefit of infusion cooking lies in how easy and convenient healthy cooking and eating are with this technique. But Glorious One-Pot Meals are only as convenient as the ingredients you have on hand, and only as nutritious as the ingredients used. Our goal is to create a pantry that is Glorious One-Pot Meal–friendly and provides you with ready ammunition for creative one-pot-meal cooking.

Let's face it, fresh meat/poultry/fish, vegetables, and herbs are preferred simply because fresh food tastes better than canned or frozen. But do you really want to hit the grocery store every few days? This requirement for healthy eating has been the bane of many an aspiring dieter or healthy eater. With a well-stocked pantry and freezer, you can avoid multiple trips to the store and still eat healthy, low-fat, and nutritious meals. And you won't have half a week's worth of vegetables rotting in the fridge to trigger guilt.

Glorious One-Pot Meal recipes begin with simple, unprocessed ingredients. By steering clear of prepackaged mixes or side dishes such as flavored rice, your food will taste better and you'll avoid putting additives, preservatives, and sodium into your body as well as help the environment by discouraging the production of wasteful packaging.

A word about food quality: Many fresh foods sold in this country are grown from genetically modified seeds with the assistance of regulated or unregulated pesticides and chemical fertilizers using unsustainable agricultural methods. The more organic foods you select, the more you minimize your intake of these toxic substances. Remember that in America we vote with our dollars, and how you spend your money directly affects the price and availability of natural foods.

Following are lists of staples and useful ingredients to have on hand in your pantry, refrigerator, or freezer. The quantities suggested supply enough for a few meals. Select a few items from each category to begin building your Glorious One-Pot Meal pantry. Refer back to the list occasionally for new ideas.

GRAINS

Invest in some kitchen canisters or plastic storage containers to store grains. You can also simply reuse mason jars by cleaning and sterilizing them in a hot water and white vinegar bath and then running them through the dishwasher. Storing grains in airtight containers helps keep freshness in and excess moisture or dryness out. Try shopping the bulk food bins in health food stores for low prices and organic options.

2 CUPS OF EACH:

Hulled barley

Pasta: orzo, penne, farfalle (bow tie)

Rice: Jasmine, sushi, Arborio, parboiled brown, and instant brown rice (parboiled and precooked)

Whole wheat couscous

Quinoa

Polenta

VEGETABLES

Keeping fresh vegetables around is always a good idea, but when you're out of them it's not a problem to resort to frozen or canned. Frozen vegetables contain fewer preservatives than canned and are usually the first-choice alternative to fresh. Some vegetables, however, like tomatoes, are best preserved by the canning process.

When buying canned or frozen vegetables, read the labels and try to purchase the least-processed brands with the lowest sodium levels and the fewest additives and preservatives. Organic brands are typically the purest and most chemical-free. Consider rinsing the canned items to remove unwanted additives.

If you find yourself with too many fresh vegetables in one week, simply wash, chop, and freeze them in a plastic container or zip-top plastic bag for later use in a Glorious One-Pot Meal. Remember that this section is not intended to guide your weekly fresh vegetable purchasing, but rather to stock up for convenient cooking.

FROZEN VEGETABLES:

Green beans
Broccoli
Corn kernels
Brussels sprouts
Spinach
Loose hash browns
Mixed vegetables

CANNED VEGETABLES:

Tomatoes (14-ounce cans)
Artichoke hearts packed in water
Black olives
Garbanzo beans (chickpeas)
Beans (black, white, pinto, etc.)

DRIED BEANS:

Lentils (about 2 cups)—store in a jar or canister.

FRESH VEGETABLES THAT STORE WELL:

Beets—store in the refrigerator crisper drawer; last a month or more.
Potatoes—white, yellow, sweet, and yams; last up to a month. Store in a cool, dry place. Do not store in the fridge.
Squash—store in a cool, dry place (not the fridge); can last for months.
Onions—store in a cool, dry place (not the fridge).

POULTRY/MEAT/FISH

When purchasing poultry, meat, and fish to freeze for future Glorious One-Pot Meals, consider the size of the pieces and how they will fit into your Dutch oven, because you won't be defrosting them before adding them to the pot. A large clump of several chicken breasts frozen together, for example, will not work well. In general, try to freeze in single-serving sizes (three to four ounces). For larger appetites, apportion four- to five-ounce servings. Freeze items individually either in zip-top freezer bags with the least amount of air possible or with a vacuum sealer for maximum freshness retention.

Since the only time a frozen ingredient may affect the baking time of a Glorious One-Pot Meal is when it contains bones, consider sticking with boneless pieces for frozen use.

Choose lean cuts of beef, lamb, or pork cut into portions that will fit into the pot without defrosting. Be sure to trim meats and poultry well before freezing because, unlike other cooking methods such as pan-frying or grilling, infusion cooking will not melt away excess fat.

Shaping ground meat into patties or meatballs before freezing allows you to toss in as much meat as you want without defrosting or hacking through a frozen mass. For better shape retention, consider adding a beaten egg and dried bread crumbs to ground meat before forming into shapes. Be sure to freeze patties or balls individually, after which they can be stored together.

People who have never liked fish may want to start with the milder flavors of white, flaky fillets of flounder, tilapia, sole, or halibut and later progress to the wonderful tastes of snapper, roughy, and catfish. Eventually you may even enjoy the heavenly aromas and flavors of perfectly infused salmon, halibut, or tuna, brimming with omega-3 essential fatty acids. Bags of unadulterated frozen fish fillets (without breading or seasoning) are inexpensive and easily found at grocery or warehouse stores.

Here are some guidelines for a well-stocked freezer:

Chicken: 4 to 6 pieces
Turkey: two 6- to 10-ounce tenderloins
Ground turkey: 6 to 10 ounces (freeze in patties or meatballs)
Beef, lamb, or pork: 4- to 6-ounce tenderloins
Ground beef: 6 to 10 ounces (freeze in patties or meatballs)
Fish: $1^{1}/2$ to 3 pounds of frozen fillets (store in a resealable freezer storage bag)

PREPARED SAUCES AND OILS

When adding prepared sauces to an infused one-pot meal, think vinaigrette rather than creamy. Not only are vinaigrettes lower in fat and calories, but both homemade and prepared vinaigrettes contain a balance of acid and alkaline that lends itself to tasty and explosive flavors.

ONE BOTTLE OR JAR:
Soy sauce
Hoisin sauce
Teriyaki sauce
Thai fish sauce
Barbecue sauce
Italian-type vinaigrette salad dressing
Balsamic, red wine, apple cider, or
   other flavored vinegars
Extra virgin olive oil
Sesame oil
Salsa

Look for oil sprays that contain pure oil and the least amount of preservatives. Try to invest in oil sprays from the health food market or purchase your own refillable oil sprayer.

ONE SPRAY CAN EACH:
Olive oil
Canola oil

HERBS AND SPICES

SALT:
I always recommend using sea salt

PEPPERS:
Black peppercorns and a grinder,
   finely ground white pepper, red pepper flakes, ground cayenne

FRESH AND/OR DRIED HERBS,
INCLUDING:
Basil, cumin (ground and seeds),
   dill, marjoram, oregano, parsley,
   rosemary, sage, thyme

PREPARED SPICE MIXTURES:
Cajun or Creole seasoning, Old Bay
   Seasoning

The Weekly Grocery List for Glorious One-Pot Meal Convenience

Use these suggestions as a basic format for weekly Glorious One-Pot Meal shopping. Be sure not to overshop for fresh items, but do try to purchase extra dry goods to build up your pantry stock. This list assumes you may prepare two or three Glorious One-Pot Meals in a week and that you will freeze what you don't use quickly.

VEGETABLES:
1 to 3 meals' worth of green (bell pepper, zucchini, spinach, green beans, Brussels sprouts, broccoli, asparagus, etc.)
1 to 3 meals' worth of red/purple (tomatoes, eggplant, beets, red bell pepper, etc.)
1 to 3 meals' worth of yellow/orange (squash, carrots, orange/yellow bell peppers, etc.)
$1/2$ pound mushrooms (any type)
1 or 2 onions (or shallots, leeks, etc.)
1 head garlic

FRUITS:
1 or 2 lemons and/or limes

POULTRY/MEAT/FISH:
2 fresh meals' worth (3 to 4 ounces per person per meal)
1 or 2 meals' worth to freeze, or as needed to regularly restock your freezer

GRAINS:
1 to 3 meals' worth of pasta, couscous, rice, barley, quinoa, or other dry goods or grains (1/2 to 1 cup uncooked per recipe)

SEASONINGS:
1 or 2 packages fresh herbs, or
1 bottle prepared marinade, or
1 other flavoring element (chili paste, spicy peanut sauce, etc.)

Nutritional Analysis Data

In truth, I believe if you stick to a diet of whole foods, you don't need to examine nutritional data, as you can be sure that what you're eating is healthy and nutritious. Additionally, I don't expect every reader to make each recipe exactly as written. A premise of this cooking method is its inherent flexibility: If a recipe calls for pork, you can alternatively make it with chicken, beef, fish, or even tofu.

Still, I know that many people routinely look at the nutritional analysis before making a dish, so as a courtesy to those of you who want it, the nutritional breakdown per serving is included for each recipe. Please consider the following disclaimer when viewing this information.

All nutritional information herein is based upon amounts designated in the recipe presented. Where items such as "chicken breasts or thighs" appear, calculations are based on an average four-ounce serving. All food calculations are derived from *The Complete Book of Food Counts* by Corinne T. Netzer (Dell Publishing, 2000). Some figures are approximate given the variation in such things as the size of vegetables, brand of broth used, and so forth. Additionally, the figures presented are rounded to the nearest whole numbers.

Since all Glorious One-Pot Meals can be altered at will, the food counts given may or may not reflect the actual meal you create at home.

FISH

Cajun Fish

In America, we're accustomed to eating sweet potatoes candied with maple syrup and brown sugar, or even topped with marshmallows, for a supersweet Thanksgiving side dish. But savory sweet potatoes are another experience entirely. Sweet potatoes with Creole seasoning are fabulous, and with this recipe they're very easy to make.

Any Cajun or Creole seasoning mix from the grocery will do, or make your own by mixing equal parts paprika, salt, and a dash of cayenne. Be careful with the cayenne, as a little goes a long way.

Beets make a delicious red substitute for tomatoes if you can't find good fresh ones for this dish. If you prefer white potatoes, feel free to substitute a large baking potato for the sweet potato. Frozen green beans are a quick solution when you want something green to toss into a pot meal. Simply shake some beans into the pot, reseal the bag, and keep it in the freezer. A single bag can often last for quite a few meals. SERVES 2

Olive or canola oil spray
1/4 medium onion, thinly sliced
1/2 to 3/4 pound white fish fillets (catfish, sole, cod, halibut, etc.)
Cajun or Creole seasoning

1 medium sweet potato, cut into 1-inch cubes
3 to 5 garlic cloves, chopped
2 cups fresh or frozen cut green beans
4 small plum tomatoes, quartered

Preheat the oven to 450°F.

Spray the inside and lid of a cast-iron Dutch oven with olive or canola oil.

Scatter the onion in the pot. Lay the fish over the onion. Sprinkle liberally with Cajun seasoning, according to taste. Remember that the spices will intensify during infusion cooking, so you may want to sprinkle lightly if you are concerned about the heat.

Layer the potato, garlic, green beans, and tomatoes, adding more seasoning as desired. Pack in as many vegetables as possible, but make sure the lid fits tightly.

Cover and bake for 35 to 45 minutes, or until 3 minutes after the aroma of a fully cooked meal escapes the oven. Serve immediately.

Dill Salmon

This is a great light summer meal! Adding a thin coating of olive oil on top of the fish will result in a less-dense fillet. For an even richer flavor, place several pats of butter on the fish. SERVES 2

Olive oil spray

2 scallions, white and green parts, chopped

$^1/_2$ to $^3/_4$ pound salmon fillet

1 teaspoon olive oil

Sea salt and freshly ground white or black pepper

3 garlic cloves, thinly sliced

$^1/_2$ lemon, thinly sliced

5 to 7 whole fresh dill sprigs

5 or 6 red potatoes, thickly sliced

2 large carrots, cut into long strips

$^1/_2$ medium zucchini, cut into sticks

1 celery stalk, sliced

$^1/_2$ medium cucumber, cut into sticks

Preheat the oven to 450°F.

Spray the inside and lid of a cast-iron Dutch oven with olive oil.

Scatter the scallions in the pot. Set the salmon on top of the scallions, skin side down if not skinned, and drizzle with olive oil. Sprinkle with salt and pepper, followed by the garlic.

Top the fillets with the lemon slices and half the dill sprigs. Scatter the potatoes around the fish. Add the carrots, zucchini, celery, and cucumber. Tuck more dill sprigs into crevices and lightly season again with salt and pepper.

Cover and bake for about 43 minutes, or until 3 minutes after the aroma of a fully cooked meal escapes the oven. Serve immediately.

CALORIES 407 • PROTEIN 30G • CARBOHYDRATES 46G • FAT 13G • CHOLESTEROL 70MG • SODIUM 113MG • FIBER 6G

Far East Fish

Vary this meal and go Italian instead with sun-dried tomato and garlic in olive oil instead of the peanut oil mixture. Or use any other type of flavored oil in this recipe. SERVES 2

Olive oil spray

3/4 cup quinoa

1 cup water, broth (chicken or vegetable), white wine, or any mixture

1/2 to 3/4 pound fish steaks (halibut, salmon, tuna, etc.)

2 tablespoons peanut oil

1 tablespoon soy sauce

1/2 teaspoon minced garlic

1/2 teaspoon red pepper flakes

1 tablespoon chopped fresh cilantro

1/2 teaspoon minced fresh ginger

1/4 head cauliflower, cut into medium florets (about 2 cups)

1 medium zucchini, halved horizontally and cut into half moons

Sea salt

6 to 8 cremini or other mushrooms, sliced

Preheat the oven to 450°F.

Spray the inside and lid of a cast-iron Dutch oven with olive oil.

Pour in the quinoa and liquid. Stir to coat the grains and make an even layer. Add the fish.

In a small bowl, mix the peanut oil, soy sauce, garlic, red pepper flakes, cilantro, and ginger. Drizzle half of this mixture over the fish. Scatter the cauliflower and zucchini over the fish. Sprinkle with salt and drizzle on the rest of the peanut oil mixture. Drop in the mushrooms.

Cover and bake for about 45 minutes, or until 3 minutes after the aroma of a fully cooked meal escapes the oven. Serve immediately.

CALORIES 489 • PROTEIN 28G • CARBOHYDRATES 52G • FAT 20G • CHOLESTEROL 31MG • SODIUM 468MG • FIBER 6G

Ed's New England Fish Chowder

Not quite a soup, New England fish chowder is known for its succulent large chunks of seafood and vegetables coated in a thin, milky broth. Traditionally this is made with cod; however, tilapia, flounder, or any other white fish will work fine. You can even use fillets directly from the freezer without defrosting them first. The fish will break into pieces as it cooks, or you can break it up while serving. Add any type of fresh or frozen seafood, such as crab or shrimp, or eight ounces of corn kernels for an even heartier meal.

The type of milk used will affect how thick the broth is. Choose skim, 2 percent, whole, soy, rice, almond, or even heavy cream to suit your preference.

To quickly remove the stems of chard (and other leafy greens like kale), hold the sides of the leaves together in one hand and use the other to rip the stem from the bottom of the leaf. Chard stems can be bitter. By chopping the stems finely and placing them on the bottom of the pot, they will have the opportunity to brown slightly and lose most of their bitterness. SERVES 2

Canola oil spray

4 Swiss chard leaves, red or green

2 medium red potatoes, halved and sliced

Sea salt and freshly ground black pepper

$^{1}/_{2}$ to $^{3}/_{4}$ pound white fish fillets (cod, flounder, tilapia, etc.)

14 ounces clams, shelled (fresh, frozen, or canned)

3 or 4 mushrooms, thinly sliced

2 tablespoons milk

1 teaspoon Old Bay Seasoning

CALORIES 255 • PROTEIN 37G • CARBOHYDRATES 18G • FAT 3G • CHOLESTEROL 77MG • SODIUM 155MG • FIBER 2G

Preheat the oven to 450°F.

Spray the inside and lid of a cast-iron Dutch oven with canola oil.

Separate the chard leaves and stems. (See headnote.) Mince the stems especially fine and spread across the bottom of the pot. Coarsely chop the leaves and reserve.

Scatter the potatoes in the pot and season with salt and pepper. Place the fish on top of the potatoes.

Drain the clams, reserving the liquid. (Frozen clams will not need to be drained.) Add the clams to the pot and top with the mushrooms.

In a small bowl, combine the milk, Old Bay Seasoning, the liquid from the clams, and salt and pepper to taste. Pour into the pot.

Pack in the chard leaves until the pot is full but the lid will still fit tightly. Cover and bake for 35 minutes, or until 3 minutes after the aroma of a fully cooked meal escapes the oven. Serve immediately.

Fish Florentine

Legend has it that when Catherine de Medici of Florence was wed to Henry of Aragon, she brought a Florentine chef with her to prepare the foods she adored. The Florentine style of cooking leans toward simple preparations of fresh foods to make consistently appealing meals. Traditionally, this dish uses a flaky white fish such as sole, cod, or halibut, but it does wonders for a salmon fillet or even orange roughy.

Pack as much spinach as possible into the pot as it will cook down significantly. Don't be afraid to push down the leaves with the heel of your hand. Just be sure that the seal around the lid is tight when the pot goes in the oven. SERVES 2

Olive oil spray

2 packed cups roughly chopped fresh spinach

1/2 to 3/4 pound fish fillets (sole, cod, halibut, salmon, etc.)

1 lemon, 1/2 thinly sliced, 1/2 cut into wedges

3 to 6 garlic cloves, sliced

2 or 3 tomatoes, thickly sliced

Grated Parmesan cheese, optional

Bread crumbs, optional

Preheat the oven to 450°F.

Spray the inside and lid of a cast-iron Dutch oven with olive oil.

Line the bottom of the pot with about half the spinach. Add the fish and spray lightly with olive oil. Cover with a single layer of lemon slices and garlic.

Layer the remaining spinach and arrange the tomato slices on top, leaving just enough room for the lid to fit securely. If desired, sprinkle lightly with Parmesan cheese or bread crumbs.

Cover and bake for 40 to 45 minutes, or until 3 minutes after the aroma of a fully cooked meal escapes the oven. Serve immediately with the lemon wedges and, if desired, sprinkle with grated Parmesan.

CALORIES 153 • PROTEIN 28G • CARBOHYDRATES 12G • FAT 2G • CHOLESTEROL 54MG • SODIUM 148MG • FIBER 2G

Fish with Herbes de Provence

The term herbes de Provence *refers to the mix of herbs commonly used in southern French cooking. These include basil, thyme, chives, oregano, sage, rosemary, lavender, and dill, and can be used in almost any combination. You can purchase a premixed jar of herbes de Provence and use that in place of the herbs designated in this recipe. Any white fish tastes great in this dish. Try this with cod, sole, roughy, or snapper.* SERVES 2

Olive oil spray

1 lemon, thinly sliced

5 garlic cloves, sliced

$^1/_2$ to $^3/_4$ pound white fish fillets

1 tablespoon fresh thyme leaves, or 1 teaspoon dried

1 tablespoon chopped fresh basil, or 1 teaspoon dried

3 or 4 fresh chives, minced

3 or 4 medium red potatoes, sliced into $^1/_2$-inch rounds

8 to 10 mushrooms, sliced

2 cups fresh or frozen cut green beans, or 1 small zucchini, sliced

1 tablespoon drained capers, optional

Preheat the oven to 450°F.

Spray the inside and lid of a cast-iron Dutch oven with olive oil. Arrange a third of the lemon and garlic slices in the bottom of the pot. Add the fish in a single layer (cut the fillets into pieces, if necessary) and top with another third of the lemon and the rest of the garlic. Sprinkle most of the herbs over the fish, keeping some in reserve.

Add the potatoes, mushrooms, and beans in layers, sprinkling with the remaining herbs, until the pot is full. Top with capers, if desired.

Cover and bake for about 45 minutes, or until 3 minutes after the aroma of a fully cooked meal escapes the oven. Serve immediately, garnished with the remaining lemon.

CALORIES 167 • PROTEIN 15G • CARBOHYDRATES 26G • FAT 2G • CHOLESTEROL 19MG • SODIUM 216MG • FIBER 2G

Fish with Hong Kong Sauce

When my husband and I were in Hong Kong on what would turn out to be our engagement trip, we became devotees of a local diner that served this ketchup-based sauce over almost anything. We Americans tend to recoil at the thought of serving the lowly condiment ketchup with anything besides hamburgers and French fries. In this recipe, ketchup is used as a subtle accent, so for the best and freshest flavor, choose a high-quality organic ketchup.

This Glorious One-Pot Meal is fabulous with a fillet of salmon or tuna, but you can use chicken or beef instead. It's hard to resist this mouthwatering sauce. Substitute any vegetables you wish; just try to provide a rainbow of green, red, and yellow vegetables to maximize nutritional value. SERVES 2

2 teaspoons sesame oil

$^1/_4$ medium onion, chopped

4 garlic cloves, minced

1 cup white rice

1 to 1$^1/_2$ teaspoons Asian chili paste

$^1/_2$ to $^3/_4$ pound fish fillets or steaks

Sea salt and freshly ground black pepper

1 tablespoon white wine or sherry

3 tablespoons ketchup, preferably organic

1 tablespoon minced fresh ginger, or $^1/_4$ teaspoon ground

1 tablespoon sugar

1 teaspoon cornstarch

2 cups fresh or frozen cut green beans

10 to 15 asparagus stalks, trimmed and cut into thirds

$^3/_4$ cup shredded red cabbage

Preheat the oven to 450°F.

Use a paper towel to wipe the inside and lid of a cast-iron Dutch oven with the sesame oil.

Spread the onion and garlic in the pot.

Add the rice to the pot with 1 cup plus 1 tablespoon water and $^1/_2$ teaspoon of the chili paste. Stir to make an even layer of the rice. Place the fish on top, skin side down. Lightly season with salt and pepper and add the wine.

In a small bowl, mix the ketchup, ginger, about $^1/_2$ teaspoon salt, the sugar, cornstarch, $^1/_2$ to 1 teaspoon chili paste, and 3 tablespoons warm water. Whisk well to dissolve all of the ingredients, especially the cornstarch.

Layer the green beans and asparagus over the fish. Drizzle half of the ketchup mixture evenly over the top. Cover with the cabbage and pour the rest of the ketchup mixture over all.

Cover and bake for 45 minutes, or until 3 minutes after the aroma of a fully cooked meal escapes the oven. Serve immediately unless the rice is still crunchy. If this is the case, remove the pot from the oven and let it sit with the lid tightly closed for an additional 5 minutes to allow the steam to penetrate the grains. Fluff the rice with a fork before serving.

Mediterranean-Style Trout

Eat in the light, clean, Mediterranean tradition for meals that are low in fat but high in flavor. Vary this recipe by using other vegetables such as eggplant, broccoli, Brussels sprouts, and mushrooms or by replacing the fish with chicken, strip steak, or even seitan (a wheat product found near the tofu in the refrigerated section of the health food store). This recipe has an elegance that will impress your guests.

I like to use an oval Dutch oven with fish fillets simply because they tend to fit better. However, to make a long fillet fit into a round pot, simply cut the fillet into two or three pieces and lay them side by side.

You can easily skip the wine in this recipe and still have a great-tasting meal, but if you do use wine, try a Chardonnay or Sauvignon Blanc that you would happily drink rather than a "cooking wine." SERVES 2

Olive oil spray
1 cup Arborio rice
$^1/_2$ to $^3/_4$ pound trout fillets
1 tablespoon drained capers
1 tablespoon chopped fresh parsley
2 to 5 garlic cloves, chopped

1 cup fresh or frozen pearl onions
$^1/_4$ cup sliced kalamata olives
1 cup fresh or frozen cut green beans
Sea salt and freshly ground black pepper
2 or 3 plum tomatoes, roughly chopped
$^1/_3$ cup white wine

CALORIES 620 • PROTEIN 33G • CARBOHYDRATES 91G • FAT 15G • CHOLESTEROL 66MG • SODIUM 538MG • FIBER 7G

Preheat the oven to 450°F.

Spray the inside and lid of a cast-iron Dutch oven with olive oil.

Rinse the rice in a strainer under cold water until the water runs clear. Tip the rice into the pot. Add 1 cup of water and stir to make an even layer. Set the trout in next, skin side down. Sprinkle the capers, half the parsley, and all the garlic over the trout.

Scatter the onions and the olives on and around the trout. Add the green beans and lightly season with salt and pepper.

Add the tomatoes, sprinkle with the rest of the parsley, and again lightly season with salt and pepper. Pour the wine over all.

Cover and bake for 45 minutes, or until 3 minutes after the aroma of a fully cooked meal escapes the oven. Serve immediately.

Garlic Fish

The first time I presented this recipe to my children, then four and two, my older son threw a fit, said it looked "disgusting," and refused to eat it. I calmly reminded him of our rule for new (or forgotten!) foods: You must eat three bites of each item and then if you still don't like anything on the plate you can have something else. Within minutes they both had polished off full plates and asked for seconds! Garlic is a favorite flavor for my kids, and when the whole garlic cloves come into contact with the spray of oil, they take on a mellow, sautéed taste. Try a less "fishy" fish for unenthusiastic fish eaters; consider sole, flounder, or tilapia. SERVES 2

Canola oil spray

8 garlic cloves

10 to 12 ounces frozen hash browns (not the patties)

Pinch of sea salt

$^1/_2$ to $^3/_4$ pound fish fillets

2 carrots, sliced into coins

$^1/_2$ head broccoli, cut into florets, or about 2 cups frozen broccoli florets

1 cup frozen corn

Preheat the oven to 450°F.

Spray the inside and lid of a cast-iron Dutch oven with canola oil.

Lay the garlic cloves in the pot.

Shake the hash browns over the bottom of the pot in a thick layer and sprinkle with salt.

Add the fish and layer the carrots, broccoli, and corn on top.

Cover and bake for 30 to 45 minutes, or until 3 minutes after the aroma of a fully cooked meal escapes the oven. Serve immediately.

CALORIES 263 • PROTEIN 21G • CARBOHYDRATES 46G • FAT 3G • CHOLESTEROL 18MG • SODIUM 91MG • FIBER 9G

Honey-Chili Trout

Almost all of the ingredients in this dish are native to North America, including the chili powder, making it a truly American dish with a hint of the Southwest. The amount of chili powder used is only enough to give the fish a little bite of heat. Add more or less according to your preference. Or use fresh, diced chiles instead.

Try this recipe with salmon, halibut, or other kinds of fish. Or substitute chicken breasts, turkey, or pork tenderloin for the fish. SERVES 2

Olive oil spray
1 cup quinoa
$1/2$ to $3/4$ pound trout fillets
1 teaspoon chili powder, or to taste
2 tablespoons honey
$1/4$ cup fresh orange juice
2 garlic cloves, chopped

$1/2$ medium zucchini, cut lengthwise and sliced into $1/2$-inch half moons
$1/2$ small yellow squash, cut lengthwise and sliced into $1/2$-inch half moons
14 ounces corn, fresh, frozen, or canned (drained)
Sea salt and freshly ground black pepper

Preheat the oven to 450°F.

Spray the inside and lid of a cast-iron Dutch oven with olive oil.

Place the quinoa in the pot with 1 cup water and stir the grains to make an even layer. Place the trout on top of the grains, skin side down.

In a small bowl, mix the chili powder, honey, orange juice, and garlic. Pour the mixture over the fish.

Scatter the zucchini and squash on top of the fish. Add the corn, filling the crevices. Season with salt and pepper.

Cover and bake for 45 minutes, or until 3 minutes after the aroma of a fully cooked meal escapes the oven. Serve immediately.

CALORIES 622 • PROTEIN 39G • CARBOHYDRATES 87G • FAT 14G • CHOLESTEROL 66MG • SODIUM 104MG • FIBER 11G

Lemon-Rosemary Salmon

This is a lovely light and flavorful recipe that's perfect for summertime dining. I have fun using pattypan squash, but any yellow summer squash will fit the bill. And if it's not asparagus season, consider substituting broccoli spears. SERVES 2

Olive oil spray

5 to 7 medium red potatoes, cut into ¹/₂-inch slices

Sea salt and freshly ground black pepper

¹/₂ to ³/₄ pound salmon fillets

Pinch of grated lemon zest, preferably from an organic lemon

4 to 5 yellow pattypan squash

7 to 10 mushrooms, thickly sliced

8 to 10 asparagus stalks

2 or 3 fresh rosemary sprigs

Preheat the oven to 450°F.

Spray the inside and lid of a cast-iron Dutch oven with olive oil.

Make a thick layer of potatoes in the pot and season lightly with salt and pepper. Lay the salmon on top. Spray the salmon with olive oil; then sprinkle the fish with lemon zest.

Trim the top and bottom of the squash and cut into wedges like a pizza. Scatter the squash in the pot, followed by the mushrooms.

Snap the tough ends from the asparagus and arrange the stalks next, topping with rosemary sprigs.

Cover and bake for about 25 minutes, or until 3 minutes after the aroma of a fully cooked meal escapes the oven. Serve immediately.

Mediterranean Red Snapper

Kalamata olives and/or capers would be lovely additions to this meal. Add them with the cherry tomatoes. You can also use a whole red snapper if you find one that fits in your Dutch oven.

I like to use canned or frozen artichoke hearts packed in water, though marinated artichoke hearts packed in herbed olive oil would add another layer of flavor to this meal. And any white wine is fine to use here. I often use a Chenin Blanc or a Sauvignon Blanc simply because those are what I like to drink. SERVES 2

Olive oil spray
1/2 cup couscous
1/2 cup white wine
1/2 to 3/4 pound red snapper fillets
1 teaspoon olive oil
1 small lemon, sliced
1/4 small red onion, sliced
2 tablespoons chopped fresh parsley

3 to 6 garlic cloves, chopped
Sea salt and freshly ground black pepper
1 cup canned or frozen artichoke hearts, halved
1/2 head broccoli, cut into florets (about 2 cups)
1 cup halved cherry tomatoes

Preheat the oven to 450°F.

Spray the inside and lid of a cast-iron Dutch oven with olive oil.

Pour the couscous into the pot. Add the wine and 1 tablespoon water and stir to coat all the grains and spread them evenly. Lay the red snapper in the pot, skin side down. Drizzle with olive oil and top with the slices of lemon and onion. Sprinkle with half of the parsley and garlic and lightly salt and pepper to taste.

Scatter in the artichoke hearts, broccoli, and tomatoes. Sprinkle with the rest of the parsley and garlic.

Cover and bake for 45 minutes, or until 3 minutes after the aroma of a fully cooked meal escapes the oven. Serve immediately.

CALORIES 466 • PROTEIN 37G • CARBOHYDRATES 65G • FAT 5G • CHOLESTEROL 42MG • SODIUM 42MG • FIBER 11G

Mango-Miso Fish

I've been finding fresh mangoes at my local grocery store often lately, but if you don't have one, use a can of puree or fresh orange juice.

If you don't have macadamia nut oil, it's okay to use another nut oil or even olive oil, but realize you will lose some depth of flavor. Vary your meal by changing the lentils: Red lentils will result in a mushier texture, while green lentils will offer a more al dente eating experience.

I like to use white or mellow-flavored miso paste, but the strength of miso flavor is really a personal preference. SERVES 2

2 teaspoons macadamia nut oil, other nut oil, or olive oil

1 cup sushi rice

$1/2$ cup dried lentils

$1^3/_4$ cups broth (chicken or vegetable) or water

2 tablespoons chopped fresh mint

$1/2$ to $3/_4$ pound fish fillets or steaks (tilapia, mahi mahi, halibut, etc.)

$1/_4$ cup fresh diced or canned pureed mango or pulpy orange juice

1 tablespoon miso paste

2 teaspoons mirin

3 tablespoons sake

Sea salt and freshly ground black pepper

1 portobello mushroom, sliced

$1/2$ red bell pepper, cored, seeded, and sliced

2 medium yellow or red tomatoes, cut into wedges

2 to 3 cups roughly chopped fresh spinach

CALORIES 295 • PROTEIN 27G • CARBOHYDRATES 42G • FAT 3G • CHOLESTEROL 19MG • SODIUM 406MG • FIBER 13G

Preheat the oven to 450°F.

Wipe the inside and lid of a cast-iron Dutch oven with macadamia nut oil.

Rinse the rice in a strainer under cold water until the water runs clear. Pour the rice and the lentils into the pot and add the liquid. Sprinkle with mint. Place the fish on top.

In a small bowl, mix the mango, miso, mirin, and sake, then pour over the fish. Lightly season with salt and pepper. Cover with the mushroom and bell pepper slices.

Arrange the tomato wedges in a layer. Top with the spinach until the pot is full.

Cover and bake for 40 to 45 minutes, or until 3 minutes after the aroma of a fully cooked meal escapes the oven. Serve immediately.

Olive and Sun-Dried Tomato Halibut

If you don't have any broth on hand, you can use plain cold water in a pinch, but using broth or bouillon makes for more flavorful couscous. Depending on your climate, oven temperature, and how thickly you sprayed the oil on the pot, the couscous may have some crunchy spots where it browned. To avoid this, spray the pot generously with oil and stir carefully to expose all the grains when adding the broth. Fluff the couscous with a fork when serving to separate the grains.

If you don't like halibut, try using salmon fillets or steaks instead. Or substitute two chicken breasts for the fish. SERVES 2

Olive oil spray

$^1/_2$ cup couscous

$^1/_2$ cup plus 1 tablespoon broth (chicken or vegetable)

Two 4- to 6-ounce halibut steaks

$^1/_3$ cup oil-packed sun-dried tomatoes, thinly sliced

2 tablespoons oil from sun-dried tomatoes or olive oil

$^1/_3$ cup pitted kalamata olives, halved

2 tablespoons drained capers

1 teaspoon dried thyme

1 tablespoon balsamic vinegar

3 garlic cloves, chopped

$^1/_2$ head broccoli, cut into florets (about 2 cups)

$^1/_2$ red bell pepper, cored, seeded, and sliced

Two 3-inch fresh rosemary sprigs

Preheat the oven to 450°F.

Spray the inside and lid of a cast-iron Dutch oven with olive oil.

Pour the couscous into the pot.

Add the broth and stir to coat the grains and spread them evenly in the pot. Arrange the halibut on top of the couscous.

CALORIES 490 • PROTEIN 19G • CARBOHYDRATES 32G • FAT 31G • CHOLESTEROL 21MG • SODIUM 121MG • FIBER 5G

In a small bowl, mix the tomatoes, the sun-dried tomato oil, olives, capers, thyme, balsamic vinegar, and garlic. Spoon half of the mixture over the halibut, taking care that most of the oil goes directly on the fish so it doesn't dry out.

Add the broccoli, then the bell pepper. Spoon the rest of the tomato mixture over all.

Tuck the sprigs of rosemary among the vegetables.

Cover and bake for 45 minutes, or until 3 minutes after the aroma of a fully cooked meal escapes the oven. Serve immediately.

Pistachio Halibut

There's something intrinsically fun about cooking with pistachios. Besides having an addictive flavor, nuts are a great source of protein and unsaturated fats. They are thought to help build and protect the nervous system, and may even help repair existing damage. As a commonsense precaution, try to avoid any red-dyed nuts.

Be sure to clean leeks thoroughly by slicing them in half lengthwise and allowing the water to sluice between the layers.

Don't expect asparagus to remain crisp in an infused one-pot meal; instead, savor the buttery softness of melt-in-your mouth stalks. SERVES 2

Olive oil spray
$^1/_2$ leek (white part), chopped
1 small sweet potato, julienned
$^1/_2$ to $^3/_4$ pound halibut fillets or steaks
1 tablespoon olive oil
$^1/_4$ cup shelled pistachios, roughly chopped
1 tablespoon chopped fresh parsley, or $^1/_2$ teaspoon dried

1 tablespoon chopped fresh marjoram or oregano, or $^1/_2$ teaspoon dried
2 teaspoons chopped fresh lavender or thyme, or $^1/_4$ teaspoon dried
1 shiitake mushroom, thinly sliced
3 cremini mushrooms, thinly sliced
4 plum tomatoes, quartered
5 to 10 thick asparagus stalks, trimmed

CALORIES 359 • PROTEIN 20G • CARBOHYDRATES 36G • FAT 16G • CHOLESTEROL 19MG • SODIUM 169MG • FIBER 7G

Preheat the oven to 450°F.

Spray the inside and lid of a cast-iron Dutch oven with olive oil.

Scatter the leek and sweet potato across the base of the pot. Place the fish on top. Drizzle the olive oil over the fish.

In a small bowl, combine the pistachios, parsley, marjoram, and lavender. Spread the mixture over the fish.

Scatter the mushrooms over and around the fish. Place the tomatoes around the pot, skin side down; top with the asparagus.

Cover and bake for about 40 minutes, or until 3 minutes after the aroma of a fully cooked meal escapes the oven. Serve immediately.

Sake-Soy Fish with Pineapple

My husband used to believe he hated pineapple because as a kid growing up in New England he ate only canned pineapple. It wasn't until he was an adult and moved west that he discovered the glory of the Hawaiian fruit. Nowadays, fresh pineapple can often be found year-round at reasonable prices in mainstream grocery stores.

Nothing compares with the taste of fresh pineapple. To peel a pineapple, chop off both ends and stand it upright. Cut the peel off with vertical strokes, then quarter the fruit from end to end. Remove the core from each quarter and discard. Lay the quarter flat and slice into wedges.

You can find sushi rice in Asian markets. SERVES 2

2 teaspoons sesame oil

1 cup sushi rice

1 cup plus 1 tablespoon broth (chicken or vegetable) or water

$^1/_2$ to $^3/_4$ pound fish (halibut, monkfish, orange roughy, or any other ocean fish)

2 tablespoons soy sauce

3 tablespoons sake

$^1/_2$ teaspoon sugar

$^1/_2$ teaspoon sambal oelek or garlic-chili paste

2 scallions, white and green parts, sliced into thin rings

2 cups diced fresh pineapple

$^1/_2$ red bell pepper, cored, seeded, and diced

$^1/_2$ orange bell pepper, cored, seeded, and diced

2 cups frozen green peas

CALORIES 701 • PROTEIN 30G • CARBOHYDRATES 116G • FAT 8G • CHOLESTEROL 18MG • SODIUM 1232MG • FIBER 16G

Preheat the oven to 450°F.

Wipe the inside and lid of a cast-iron Dutch oven with sesame oil.

Rinse the rice in a strainer under cold water until the water runs clear. Tip the rice into the pot, add the liquid, and stir to make an even layer. Add the fish.

In a small bowl, combine the soy sauce, sake, sugar, and sambal oelek. Stir until the sugar dissolves. Spread over the fish.

Sprinkle with scallions and cover with the pineapple.

Follow with the bell peppers and then the peas.

Cover and bake for 45 minutes, or until 3 minutes after the aroma of a fully cooked meal escapes the oven. Serve immediately.

Salmon with Capers

There is a big difference between farm-raised and wild salmon in taste, price, and environmental impact. Some salmon farms feed their fish antibiotics and antiparasitic medications, and even dye the salmon pink. It is always worth investigating the production methods of the food you eat so that you can make informed decisions about what goes in your body and what industries to support with your food dollars.

Italian roasted red peppers are sold by the jar and often packed in olive oil. Look for them in specialty delis and better grocery stores. SERVES 2

Olive oil spray
$^1/_2$ to $^3/_4$ pound salmon fillets, preferably wild salmon
Sea salt and freshly ground black pepper
4 garlic cloves, finely chopped
1 teaspoon drained capers

4 ounces Italian roasted red peppers, cut into pieces
$^1/_2$ cup white wine
6 to 8 small new potatoes
$^1/_2$ head broccoli, cut into florets (about 2 cups)

Preheat the oven to 450°F.

Spray the inside and lid of a cast-iron Dutch oven with olive oil.

Place the salmon in the bottom of the pot, skin side down. Spray the fillets lightly with olive oil, then season with salt and pepper to taste.

Sprinkle with the garlic and capers, scatter on the peppers, and add half the wine.

Pierce each potato multiple times with a fork and drop into the pot (if they are large, slice them into chunks). Season lightly with salt and pepper.

Add the broccoli and arrange to fit snugly inside the pot. Pour in the rest of the wine.

Cover and bake for 45 minutes, or until 3 minutes after the aroma of a fully cooked meal escapes the oven. Serve immediately.

CALORIES 414 • PROTEIN 29G • CARBOHYDRATES 43G • FAT 10G • CHOLESTEROL 70MG • SODIUM 246MG • FIBER 4G

Soy-Miso Fish

. . . .

One of my friends once owned a place that served delectable organic small plates in a funky part of town. I had a melt-in-your-mouth soy-miso monkfish that was just to die for. I've tried to re-create the experience here. Because monkfish can be hard to find, I use flounder to make this at home, but feel free to use sole, tilapia, salmon, or any fish. For that matter, this would be delicious with chicken or pork tenderloin as well.

To make the dish spicier, double or triple the amount of black bean sauce. You can usually find black bean and garlic sauce in the Asian section of the grocery store. SERVES 2

2¹/2 teaspoons sesame oil

1 cup sushi rice

¹/2 to ³/4 pound fish fillets

2 tablespoons reduced-sodium soy sauce

4 teaspoons miso paste

2 teaspoons rice wine vinegar

1 teaspoon black bean and garlic sauce

1 large golden or red beet, peeled or not and sliced

2 shiitake mushrooms, halved and sliced

2 cups snow peas

Preheat the oven to 450°F.

Wipe the inside and lid of a cast-iron Dutch oven with 2 teaspoons of the sesame oil.

Rinse the rice in a strainer until the water runs clear. Add to the pot with 1 cup plus 1 tablespoon water and stir until the rice settles into a smooth layer. Add the fish.

In a small bowl, combine the soy sauce, miso paste, rice wine vinegar, black bean and garlic sauce, and the remaining ¹/2 teaspoon of sesame oil. Stir until the miso is dissolved and the sesame oil is incorporated, then drizzle half of the mixture over the fish.

Arrange the beet slices in a layer on the fish, then scatter the mushrooms on top. Load in the snow peas and drizzle the rest of the soy mixture over all.

Cover and bake for about 45 minutes, or until 3 minutes after the aroma of a fully cooked meal escapes the oven. Serve immediately.

CALORIES 542 • PROTEIN 34G • CARBOHYDRATES 91G • FAT 3G • CHOLESTEROL 54MG • SODIUM 1371MG • FIBER 7G

Sesame Tuna with Orange Sauce

I keep individually wrapped boneless tuna steaks in the freezer just for meals like this. Just pull out the frozen steak and put it directly into the pot. There's no need to thaw and it won't add any cooking time. You can make this meal with salmon or halibut, but also with pork, turkey, or almost any kind of steak. It would also be great with shrimp or scallops for another kind of seafood dish.

To toast sesame seeds, simply scatter them on a sheet pan and place in the oven while it is preheating. Shake the pan once or twice after a few minutes and keep a close eye on the seeds, as they will burn quickly. SERVES 2

4 teaspoons sesame oil

$1/2$ cup couscous

$1/2$ cup plus 1 tablespoon broth (chicken or vegetable) or water

Two 4-ounce tuna steaks

Zest and juice of $1/2$ orange, or $1/4$ cup orange juice

2 teaspoons honey

3 tablespoons soy sauce

4 to 6 garlic cloves, chopped

2 tablespoons sesame seeds, toasted

1 teaspoon grated fresh ginger

$1/2$ head broccoli, cut into florets (about 2 cups)

1 small yellow squash, thinly sliced

CALORIES 475 • PROTEIN 38G • CARBOHYDRATES 51G • FAT 14G • CHOLESTEROL 43MG • SODIUM 1286MG • FIBER 7G

Preheat the oven to 450°F.

Coat the inside and lid of a cast-iron Dutch oven with 2 teaspoons of the sesame oil.

Pour the couscous and liquid into the pot and stir to make a smooth layer.

Add the tuna steaks in a single layer (it is okay if they are partially or completely submerged) and drizzle with 1 teaspoon of the sesame oil.

In a small bowl, whisk the orange zest, orange juice, honey, soy sauce, remaining sesame oil, garlic, sesame seeds, and ginger until thoroughly combined. Pour half the mixture over the tuna.

Add the broccoli and squash and pour the rest of the mixture over all.

Cover and bake for 45 minutes, or until 3 minutes after the aroma of a fully cooked meal escapes the oven. Serve immediately.

Sesame-Soy Salmon

The avocados in this recipe offer a cool, smooth counterpart to the spiciness of the fish and the rice. Even though they have been cooked with the rest of the meal, they maintain their shape and flavor delightfully. If you have space in your Dutch oven, try adding a handful of snow peas and sliced shiitake mushrooms to round out this Asian-inspired meal.

While using plain water will result in a wonderful meal, you can add more depth of flavor by substituting broth. The rice will completely absorb the liquid during cooking, and in the process the fish will take on a delicate, poached texture that is a treat to eat. If you live in a dry climate, you may want to add an extra 2 tablespoons of water. SERVES 2

$2^1/_2$ teaspoons sesame oil or canola oil spray

1 cup jasmine rice

$^1/_2$ to $^3/_4$ pound salmon fillet or steak

2 carrots, julienned

2 tablespoons soy sauce

1 teaspoon rice wine vinegar

$^1/_8$ teaspoon sugar

1 teaspoon grated fresh ginger

2 garlic cloves, minced

1 teaspoon red pepper flakes

$^1/_2$ teaspoon sesame seeds

1 tablespoon fresh lemon juice

$^1/_4$ head red cabbage, shredded (about 2 cups)

1 avocado, sliced

Preheat the oven to 450°F.

Coat the inside and lid of a cast-iron Dutch oven with 2 teaspoons of the sesame oil or spray with canola oil.

Rinse the rice in a strainer under cold water until the water runs clear. Tip the rice into the pot. Add 1 cup plus 1 tablespoon water and stir to make an even layer. Place the salmon in the pot and scatter the carrots on top of the fish.

In a small bowl, mix the remaining sesame oil, the soy sauce, vinegar, sugar, ginger, garlic, red pepper flakes, sesame seeds, and lemon juice. Stir until the sugar is dissolved. Pour half of the mixture into the pot.

Layer in the cabbage and top with the avocado.

Pour the rest of the soy sauce mixture over the top.

Cover and bake for 45 minutes, or until 3 minutes after the aroma of a fully cooked meal escapes the oven. Serve immediately.

Tandoori Salmon with Kale

Garam masala is the basic mix of Indian spices. You can purchase it at ethnic or health food stores. Use your favorite chile pepper in this dish. Jalapeños work fine, as do Anaheim or other green chiles, or even red pepper flakes if that's what you have in your cupboard.

For additional garnishing, use sprigs of fresh mint or cilantro. If your diet is dairy-free, try this recipe with plain soy yogurt. SERVES 2

Canola oil spray

1 cup basmati rice

1 cup broth (chicken or vegetable)

1 cup stemmed and shredded kale (see page 30)

$1/2$ to $3/4$ pound salmon fillet

1 lemon, halved

Sea salt and freshly ground black pepper

1 cup plain yogurt (regular, low-fat, or nonfat)

$1^1/2$ tablespoons grated fresh ginger

4 garlic cloves, crushed

1 small chile pepper, stemmed, seeded, and chopped

1 teaspoon garam masala

1 teaspoon ground turmeric

$1/2$ butternut squash, peeled or not and cubed (about 2 cups)

CALORIES 643 • PROTEIN 39G • CARBOHYDRATES 100G • FAT 12G • CHOLESTEROL 80MG • SODIUM 585MG • FIBER 4G

Preheat the oven to 450°F.

Spray the inside and lid of a cast-iron Dutch oven with canola oil.

Rinse the rice in a strainer under cold water until the water runs clear. Tip the rice into the pot. Add the broth and 2 tablespoons of water and stir to make an even layer.

Press the kale into the pot, mashing down until it fits below the halfway point.

Place the salmon on top of the kale. Squeeze the juice from one lemon half and drizzle over the fish. Lightly season with salt and pepper.

In a small bowl, mix the yogurt, ginger, garlic, chile pepper, garam masala, and turmeric, then pour the mixture over the salmon.

Toss in the butternut squash and lightly season with salt and pepper.

Cover and bake for 35 to 45 minutes, or until 3 minutes after the aroma of a fully cooked meal escapes the oven. Slice the other lemon half into wedges for garnish. Serve immediately.

Very, Very Mild Fish

My young children won't eat the scallions in this recipe, so I leave them whole and remove them before serving. But I'm nonetheless pleased to know I've added another flavor to their taste memory that will increase the spectrum of their eating preferences and habits over a lifetime.

The mildest types of fish—and thus more acceptable to non-fish or picky eaters—are the flat white fish: flounder, sole, even haddock or tilapia. This is one time when it is okay if the pieces of fish overlap or are even frozen together.

It is rare for me to use butter in a recipe, but in this particular case I think it gives the fish a smoother mouth experience, which might be less offensive for difficult or timid eaters. You certainly can use olive oil, or just skip it altogether. SERVES 2

Olive oil spray

1 medium russet potato, cut into small cubes

Sea salt

$^1/_2$ to $^3/_4$ pound fish fillets

3 to 4 garlic cloves, roughly chopped

1 tablespoon butter, slivered

1 thick lemon slice, or $^1/_2$ teaspoon fresh lemon juice

4 to 6 mushrooms, thickly sliced, optional

2 whole scallions, optional

2 cups baby carrots, sliced into thirds

$^1/_4$ head cauliflower, cut into bite-size florets (about 2 cups)

CALORIES 312 • PROTEIN 19G • CARBOHYDRATES 50G • FAT 10G • CHOLESTEROL 34MG • SODIUM 125MG • FIBER 10G

Preheat the oven to 450°F.

Spray the inside and lid of a cast-iron Dutch oven with olive oil.

Spread the potato evenly in the pot and season lightly with salt. Add the fish fillets. Sprinkle with the garlic, add salt to taste, and dot with the butter.

Squeeze the lemon over the fish and add the optional mushrooms. Lay the scallions, if using, atop the fish. Add the carrots and cauliflower, and season lightly with salt.

Cover and bake for about 45 minutes, or until 3 minutes after the aroma of a fully cooked meal escapes the oven. Serve immediately.

Yucatán Fish

Throughout the 1980s, my family vacationed in Cozumel, off the coast of the Yucatán Peninsula in Mexico. This recipe was one of our favorite local dishes prepared by the descendants of the Mayan Indians. Corn, peppers, and limes are all native to the New World and were likely cultivated by the ancient Mayans much as they are today. Spice up this dish with red pepper flakes or chopped chiles.

Try a white, flaky fish such as cod, flounder, or sole. Or try a slightly meatier white fish like Oreo Dory, tilapia, mahi mahi, or snapper. Either fresh or frozen fish fillets work fine. This recipe is also wonderful with seafood such as shrimp or with thin slices of flank steak or pork. SERVES 2

Canola oil spray
1/2 medium yellow onion, halved and thinly sliced
3/4 cup quinoa
1 cup broth (chicken or vegetable) or water
1/2 to 3/4 pound fish fillets
Sea salt and freshly ground black pepper
1/2 lemon, sliced in 1/4-inch rounds
1/2 lime, sliced in 1/4-inch rounds

1/2 medium red bell pepper, cored, seeded, and cut into 1/2-inch slices
1/2 medium green bell pepper, cored, seeded, and cut into 1/2-inch slices
1/2 medium yellow or orange bell pepper, cored, seeded, and cut into 1/2-inch slices
10 to 14 ounces corn, fresh, frozen, or canned (drained)
4 to 6 small tomatoes, sliced

CALORIES 442 • PROTEIN 29G • CARBOHYDRATES 70G • FAT 7G • CHOLESTEROL 37MG • SODIUM 177MG • FIBER 9G

Preheat the oven to 450°F.

Spray the inside and lid of a cast-iron Dutch oven with canola oil.

Scatter the onion over the bottom of the pot.

Add the quinoa and pour in the liquid, then stir to settle the grains evenly. Add the fish and lightly season with salt and pepper.

Alternate the lemons and limes in a single layer on top of the fish. Top with the bell pepper slices and lightly season with salt and pepper, then sprinkle on the corn. Layer the tomato slices on top and season lightly with salt and pepper.

Cover and bake for 30 to 45 minutes, or until 3 minutes after the aroma of a fully cooked meal escapes the oven. Serve immediately.

SEAFOOD

Cioppino (Seafood Stew)

Cioppino, or fisherman's stew, had its origins in San Francisco by way of Italy, but all Mediterranean countries have similar fish stews. Make this version your own with your favorite treats from the sea.

Traditionally, this dish is not very soupy; for more broth, do not drain the can of tomatoes.

I prefer to avoid precooked seafood for Glorious One-Pot Meals. If your frozen shrimp is pink, it's precooked. While using precooked seafood certainly won't ruin your meal (it's difficult to fail with a Glorious One-Pot Meal!), raw seafood results in a stronger flavor and will be more tender after cooking. SERVES 2

Olive oil spray

1 cup rotini (corkscrew pasta)

$^1/_2$ teaspoon olive oil

$^1/_2$ pound (10 to 12) shrimp, peeled and deveined

$^1/_4$ pound bay or sea scallops

Sea salt and freshly ground black pepper

$^1/_2$ medium onion, diced

3 to 5 garlic cloves, sliced or crushed

$^1/_2$ red bell pepper, cored, seeded, and cut into 1-inch slices

$^1/_2$ yellow bell pepper, cored, seeded, and cut into 1-inch slices

$^1/_2$ zucchini, halved lengthwise and cut into $^1/_2$-inch slices

One 14-ounce can diced tomatoes, drained, or 3 to 4 medium fresh tomatoes, chopped

1 celery stalk, thinly sliced

1 fennel bulb, trimmed and chopped

CALORIES 241 • PROTEIN 18G • CARBOHYDRATES 35G • FAT 3G • CHOLESTEROL 53MG • SODIUM 531MG • FIBER 5G

Preheat the oven to 450°F.

Spray the inside and lid of a cast-iron Dutch oven with olive oil.

Scatter the pasta in the pot. Add $^1/_3$ cup of water and the olive oil. Stir gently to coat the noodles and distribute evenly.

Spread the shrimp and scallops in a layer on top of the pasta. Season with salt and pepper to taste.

Scatter the onion and garlic over the seafood, followed by layers of bell peppers and zucchini.

Arrange the tomatoes in a layer on top of the zucchini.

Scatter the celery and the fennel on top, and lightly season with salt and pepper.

Cover and bake for 45 minutes, or until 3 minutes after the aroma of a fully cooked meal escapes the oven. Serve immediately.

Feta Shrimp with Roasted Tomatoes

In this recipe I deviate from the usual formula where the spinach would be the last ingredient added. I do this because sometimes spinach that touches the lid becomes browned, and although this doesn't bother me, some may find it unappetizing. This method leaves the spinach greener.

I get the best results when using frozen raw shrimp, though thawed raw shrimp will work well, too.

SERVES 2

Olive oil spray

One 14-ounce can fire-roasted tomatoes

$^1/_2$ cup couscous

2 cups roughly chopped fresh spinach, or one 10-ounce package frozen

$^1/_2$ to $^3/_4$ pound shrimp, peeled and deveined

$^1/_4$ cup chopped fresh parsley

1 tablespoon fresh lemon juice

$^1/_3$ cup feta cheese, crumbled

$^1/_2$ medium zucchini, halved lengthwise and cut into $^1/_2$-inch slices

CALORIES 349 • PROTEIN 20G • CARBOHYDRATES 49G • FAT 7G • CHOLESTEROL 63MG • SODIUM 846MG • FIBER 6G

Preheat the oven to 450°F.

Spray the inside and lid of a cast-iron Dutch oven with olive oil.

Drain the tomatoes into a measuring cup. Add water if necessary to get $1/2$ cup of liquid. Reserve the tomatoes.

Pour the couscous into the pot and add the tomato liquid. Stir to coat each grain and make an even layer.

Pack the spinach into the pot. (If using frozen spinach, break apart the block.)

In a medium bowl, stir together the tomatoes, shrimp, parsley, lemon juice, and feta, and add to the pot.

Arrange the zucchini slices on top.

Cover and bake for about 45 minutes, or until 3 minutes after the aroma of a fully cooked meal escapes the oven. Serve immediately.

New World Shrimp

. . . .

Quinoa (pronounced KEEN-wah) was an ancient staple grain of the Incas. It's a complete protein with all essential amino acids and more calcium than milk, along with iron, phosphorus, and vitamins B and E. Use it as a grain and substitute freely for rice or pasta. Just be sure to maintain the proper ratio of dry grain to liquid (for quinoa use $^3/_4$ cup quinoa to 1 cup liquid). I buy quinoa from the bulk food bins at the health food store, although you can find it at many supermarkets alongside the grains.

Raw seafood is always preferable when making a Glorious One-Pot Meal, and frozen shellfish is less likely to overcook in this method. I keep a bag of uncooked shrimp in my freezer for just such a reason. SERVES 2

Olive oil spray
$^3/_4$ cup quinoa
1 cup broth (chicken or vegetable) or water
4 to 6 garlic cloves, chopped
$^1/_2$ teaspoon dried thyme
$^1/_8$ teaspoon sea salt
1 tablespoon olive oil
$^1/_4$ cup dry vermouth or dry white wine

$^1/_2$ to $^3/_4$ pound medium raw, frozen shrimp, peeled and deveined
2 to 3 medium tomatoes, chopped, or one 14-ounce can, drained and chopped
1 green bell pepper, cored, seeded, and sliced
1 teaspoon lemon zest
$^1/_4$ teaspoon dried parsley, or 2 tablespoons chopped fresh

CALORIES 458 • PROTEIN 25G • CARBOHYDRATES 64G • FAT 12G • CHOLESTEROL 84MG • SODIUM 218MG • FIBER 7G

Preheat the oven to 450°F.

Spray the inside and lid of a cast-iron Dutch oven with olive oil.

Pour the quinoa into the pot and add the liquid. Stir to make an even layer.

In a medium bowl, mix the garlic, thyme, salt, olive oil, and vermouth. Add the shrimp and stir to coat. Pour the entire mixture into the pot.

Layer in the tomatoes and the bell pepper slices. Sprinkle with lemon zest and parsley.

Cover and bake for 45 minutes, or until 3 minutes after the aroma of a fully cooked meal escapes the oven. Remove the cover and let sit for 2 to 5 minutes before serving to allow the quinoa to fully absorb all the liquid.

Pacific Island Seafood

Adapted from a recipe out of Guam, the bananas give this meal a tropical flavor that my mother and mother-in-law both love. Be sure to cut any brown spots off the bananas before slicing.

Sweet potatoes and yams range tremendously in size. You may be able to use all of a medium sweet potato in a single meal. However, if it is ten inches or longer, use only part of it.

To make this dish even spicier, add a diced fresh jalapeño or serrano pepper to the onion layer at the bottom. SERVES 2

Canola oil spray

$^1/_4$ medium onion, thinly sliced

4 to 6 garlic cloves, chopped or crushed

1 tablespoon grated fresh ginger

1 medium or $^1/_2$ large sweet potato, halved lengthwise and cut into $^1/_4$-inch slices

$^1/_2$ to $^3/_4$ pound shrimp or scallops

2 bananas, cut into $^1/_4$-inch slices

$^1/_2$ green bell pepper, cored, seeded, and cut into thin strips

2 teaspoons sugar

$^1/_2$ teaspoon red pepper flakes

2 tablespoons white or wine vinegar

Sea salt and freshly ground black pepper

1 handful fresh spinach, or about 5 ounces frozen

One 14-ounce can diced tomatoes, drained, or 2 medium tomatoes, chopped

CALORIES 281 • PROTEIN 11G • CARBOHYDRATES 57G • FAT 2G • CHOLESTEROL 43MG • SODIUM 317MG • FIBER 8G

Preheat the oven to 450°F.

Spray the inside and lid of a cast-iron Dutch oven with canola oil.

Scatter the onion in the pot. Sprinkle with the garlic and ginger. Cover with the sweet potato slices.

Arrange the shrimp or scallops in an even layer. Cover with the bananas, and tuck the bell pepper strips among the bananas.

In a measuring cup, mix $1/4$ tablespoon water with the sugar, red pepper flakes, and vinegar. Stir until the sugar is dissolved and season lightly with salt and pepper to taste. Pour half of the mixture evenly over the bananas and peppers.

Create a layer of spinach and top with the tomatoes. Pour the rest of the seasoned water over all.

Cover and bake for 25 minutes, or until 3 minutes after the aroma of a fully cooked meal escapes the oven. Serve immediately.

Penne Puttanesca

Puttanesca is a traditional pasta dish that supposedly had its origins in the food prostitutes cooked for themselves at the end of the night. The amount of spice called for here makes a medium-spicy dish. Adjust it according to your own taste. Although anchovy paste (or minced anchovies) is called for, don't worry if you don't have any or just want to leave it out.

A tip: Do not lift the lid "just to check" before this meal is done or it will take longer to cook and your pasta may not come out perfectly al dente. This recipe works equally well with fresh or frozen shrimp. Instead of broccoli and artichoke hearts, try this with spinach or green beans. Consider red bell peppers, zucchini, yellow squash, or eggplant as well. SERVES 2

Olive oil spray

1 cup penne

$1/2$ teaspoon olive oil

$1/2$ to $3/4$ pound shrimp, peeled and deveined

4 to 6 garlic cloves, minced

1 tablespoon drained capers

1 teaspoon red pepper flakes

One 6-ounce can pitted black olives

14 ounces artichoke hearts, canned or frozen, halved

$1/2$ head broccoli, cut into florets, or 2 cups frozen

3 tablespoons chopped fresh parsley

1 teaspoon anchovy paste, or 2 to 4 minced anchovies

One 14-ounce can diced tomatoes, drained

Preheat the oven to 450°F.

Spray the inside and lid of a cast-iron Dutch oven with olive oil.

Scatter the pasta in the pot. Add $^1/_3$ cup water with the olive oil and stir gently to evenly coat and distribute the pasta.

Arrange the shrimp on top of the pasta. Sprinkle on the garlic, capers, and red pepper flakes.

Scatter the olives over the shrimp. Make a layer of the artichokes and then the broccoli. Sprinkle with the parsley.

Mix the anchovy paste with the tomatoes and pour over all.

Cover and bake for 45 minutes, or until 3 minutes after the aroma of a fully cooked meal escapes the oven. Serve immediately.

Scallops and Sweet Potatoes

The sweet potatoes soften in the broth to emerge creamy and bursting with flavor. Even though this exciting meal doesn't contain chile peppers, ginger adds considerable zing. Be careful not to overdo the black pepper as it will intensify during cooking.

Chanterelle or hedgehog wild mushrooms heighten the flavor in this dish, but shiitake or button mushrooms will taste good in a pinch.

To make julienne sticks, cut the potato into thin disks. Stack the disks and cut into thin sticks lengthwise. SERVES 2

Canola oil spray

1 small sweet potato or yam, julienned

2 or 3 shallots, or $^1/_4$ medium onion, chopped

Sea salt and freshly ground black pepper

5 to 7 mushrooms, preferably wild

$^1/_2$ to $^3/_4$ pound sea or bay scallops, fresh or frozen

4 to 7 garlic cloves, chopped

1 tablespoon grated fresh ginger, or $^1/_2$ teaspoon ground

1 tablespoon chopped fresh chives

$^1/_3$ cup broth (chicken or vegetable)

2 cups fresh or frozen green beans, cut in 2-inch lengths, or broccoli florets (about 2 cups)

Juice of $^1/_4$ lemon (about 1 teaspoon)

CALORIES 218 • PROTEIN 25G • CARBOHYDRATES 170G • FAT 2G • CHOLESTEROL 41MG • SODIUM 419MG • FIBER 5G

Preheat the oven to 450°F.

Spray the inside and lid of a cast-iron Dutch oven with canola oil.

Scatter the sweet potato in the pot.

Sprinkle on the shallots and lightly season with salt and pepper. Scatter on the mushrooms.

Arrange the scallops on top and lightly season with salt and pepper. Sprinkle on the garlic, ginger, and chives and pour the broth over all.

Add the green beans and drizzle with lemon juice.

Cover and bake for 40 minutes, or until 3 minutes after the aroma of a fully cooked meal escapes the oven. Serve immediately.

Scallops with Red and Yellow Peppers

I love the rich, decadent sensation of scallops in my mouth, but you can make this recipe with any kind of seafood, fish, or poultry. For a south-of-the-border kick, add a tablespoon of tequila to the sauce mixture and sprinkle with a tablespoon of chopped cilantro before adding the spinach.

Be sure to liberally coat the inside of the lid with oil so that the spinach will not dry out and stick. SERVES 2

Olive oil spray

4 garlic cloves, chopped

1 medium potato, peeled or not, thinly sliced

$^1/_2$ to $^3/_4$ pound sea or bay scallops

Sea salt and freshly ground black pepper

$^1/_2$ red bell pepper, cored, seeded, and thinly sliced

$^1/_2$ yellow bell pepper, cored, seeded, and thinly sliced

$^1/_4$ cup white wine

2 teaspoons balsamic vinegar

2 tablespoons honey

$^1/_4$ cup broth (chicken or vegetable) or water

$^1/_2$ teaspoon red pepper flakes

2 cups roughly chopped fresh spinach

CALORIES 314 • PROTEIN 32G • CARBOHYDRATES 39G • FAT 2G • CHOLESTEROL 58MG • SODIUM 495MG • FIBER 3G

Preheat the oven to 450°F.

Spray the inside and lid of a cast-iron Dutch oven with olive oil.

Sprinkle half the garlic in the pot. Arrange the potato slices in an overlapping pattern.

Place the scallops on the potatoes and lightly season with salt and pepper. Scatter on the bell peppers.

In a small bowl, mix the wine, vinegar, honey, broth, red pepper flakes, and the rest of the garlic. Pour over all.

Fill up the rest of the pot with spinach.

Cover and bake for 35 minutes, or until 3 minutes after the aroma of a fully cooked meal escapes the oven. Serve immediately.

Shrimp Masala with Rice

Traditional masala spices are dry-roasted, which releases the aroma. Masala also calls for pureeing the onions and tomatoes together in a blender with the yogurt mixture. Here I offer a simplified masala, designed to be quick and easy. Of course, you may always vary any recipe to suit your own preferences.

You can purchase masala spice mix in a specialty food store, or you can make your own. Combine $^1/_4$ teaspoon garam masala, $^1/_4$ teaspoon curry powder, $^1/_4$ teaspoon ground coriander, $^1/_8$ teaspoon turmeric, and $^1/_8$ teaspoon cayenne. Keep leftover mix tightly covered in a dark cabinet.

Substituting soy yogurt or light coconut milk is fine. Coconut milk used to get a bad rap for being high in saturated fat, but now we know it has the good kind of saturated fat.

Turmeric is an anti-inflammatory herb, thought to be good for diseases that cause internal swelling, such as multiple sclerosis, fibromyalgia, and arthritis. SERVES 2

Canola oil spray

$^1/_4$ medium onion, chopped

1 cup basmati rice

$^3/_4$ pound fresh or frozen shrimp, peeled and deveined

4 garlic cloves, minced or crushed

$^1/_4$ cup plain yogurt (regular, low-fat, or nonfat)

One 14-ounce can coconut milk (regular or light)

2 tablespoons chopped fresh cilantro

2 scallions, white and green parts, sliced into thin rings

$^1/_4$ teaspoon fresh lemon juice

1 teaspoon masala spice mix (see headnote)

$^1/_2$ yellow bell pepper, cored, seeded, and cut into 1-inch squares

2 cups fresh or frozen cut green beans

One 14-ounce can diced tomatoes, drained, or 3 medium tomatoes, diced

CALORIES 769 • PROTEIN 23G • CARBOHYDRATES 93G • FAT 33G • CHOLESTEROL 67MG • SODIUM 561MG • FIBER 7G

Preheat the oven to 450°F.

Spray the inside and lid of a cast-iron Dutch oven with canola oil.

Scatter the onion in the pot.

Rinse the rice in a strainer under cold water until the water runs clear. Add the rice to the pot and with the back of the spoon smooth the rice in an even layer over the onion.

Add the shrimp in a layer and sprinkle with garlic.

In a small bowl, combine the yogurt, coconut milk, cilantro, scallions, and lemon juice with the masala spice mix. Pour half of the mixture over the shrimp.

Add the bell pepper, green beans, and tomatoes. Pour the rest of the yogurt mixture over all.

Cover, place the pot on a cookie sheet to catch any overflow, and bake for 45 minutes, or until 3 minutes after the aroma of a fully cooked meal escapes the oven. Serve immediately.

Mojo Shrimp

The flavors here remind me of Jamaica, luring me in with the sweet citrus and then kicking it up with the chile peppers. SERVES 2

Olive oil spray

1 medium sweet potato, cut into julienne strips

$^1/_2$ to $^3/_4$ pound shrimp, peeled and deveined

$^1/_2$ cup fresh orange juice

2 tablespoons fresh lime juice

1 tablespoon chopped fresh oregano

1 teaspoon paprika

$^1/_2$ teaspoon red pepper flakes

$^1/_2$ teaspoon allspice

4 to 6 garlic cloves, chopped

$^1/_4$ teaspoon sea salt

$^1/_2$ medium zucchini, halved lengthwise and cut into $^1/_2$-inch slices

2 bananas, sliced $^1/_2$ inch thick

$^1/_2$ orange bell pepper, cored, seeded, and sliced

Preheat the oven to 450°F.

Spray the inside and lid of a cast-iron Dutch oven with olive oil.

Scatter the sweet potato in the pot. Add the shrimp.

In a small bowl, mix the orange juice, lime juice, oregano, paprika, red pepper flakes, allspice, garlic, and salt.

Pour half of the mixture over the shrimp.

Add the zucchini and the bananas. Top with the bell pepper slices.

Pour the rest of the orange juice mixture over all.

Cover and bake for about 40 minutes, or until 3 minutes after the aroma of a fully cooked meal escapes the oven. Serve immediately.

CALORIES 238 • PROTEIN 9G • CARBOHYDRATES 51G • FAT 2G • CHOLESTEROL 43MG • SODIUM 280MG • FIBER 6G

MEAT

Adobo Pork

Adobo, or roasted, pork is a staple in Latin America and some parts of Southeast Asia. This is just one version of the Latin American–style dish, made easier as a Glorious One-Pot Meal. Replace the rice and broth with $3/4$ cup of quinoa and 1 cup of broth for a more authentic South American meal.

Ancho chiles are actually dried poblano chiles, which are rich in flavor and popular for cooking. They've been described as looking and tasting like prunes, though certainly with more of a bite. Anaheim chiles are a milder substitute.

You can use boneless frozen pork chops without increasing the cooking time. However, if they are frozen with the bone in, you may need to allow ten extra minutes in the oven. You can also substitute flank steaks or chicken pieces with good results.

I like to add a sliced fresh tomato to this recipe. Layer the sliced tomato on top if there is still space in the pot after adding the green pepper. SERVES 2

Canola oil spray

1 cup Arborio rice

1 cup plus 2 tablespoons broth (beef, chicken, or vegetable) or water

2 ancho chiles, stemmed, seeded, and chopped

$1/4$ large onion, chopped

$1/2$ teaspoon dried oregano

$1/4$ teaspoon ground cumin

$1/2$ teaspoon freshly ground black pepper

$1/4$ teaspoon ground allspice

2 tablespoons cider vinegar

$1/4$ cup fresh orange juice

2 teaspoons fresh lime juice

$1/2$ to $3/4$ pound center-cut and deboned pork chops, 1 inch thick

One 15-ounce can corn, drained

1 green bell pepper, cored, seeded, and cut into 1-inch strips

Preheat the oven to 450°F.

Spray the inside and lid of a cast-iron Dutch oven with canola oil.

Rinse the rice in a strainer under cold water until the water runs clear. Tip the rice into the pot. Add the liquid, reserving 1 tablespoon, and stir to make an even layer.

In a small bowl, stir together the remaining 1 tablespoon of broth with the chiles, onion, oregano, cumin, pepper, allspice, vinegar, and orange and lime juices.

Place the pork chops in the pot and pour half of the mixture over them. Add the corn and bell pepper and pour in the rest of the spice mixture.

Cover and bake for 45 minutes, or until 3 minutes after the aroma of a fully cooked meal escapes the oven. Serve immediately.

All-American Pot Roast

The thinner the slice of meat, the more tender the pot roast will be. Ask your butcher to slice it less than two inches thick. Also, go for a better-quality meat for a more tender result, but be aware that it is easy to end up with tough meat if it's left in the oven too long. For rarer meat, cut the vegetables into smaller cubes ($1/2$ to 1 inch) and remove the pot from the oven at the first whiff of the robust aroma of a fully cooked meal.

To speed up your prep time, use frozen green beans and peeled baby carrots. I never peel my potatoes because so much nutrition is in the skin. Just be sure to scrub them well and dig out the eyes. I also think wild mushrooms add a wonderful depth to the meat. Try morels, chanterelles, or shiitakes.

My aunt swears by kosher salt and freshly cracked black pepper with beef. Consider both, but remember that kosher salt is more intense, so you may want to use less than you normally do.

SERVES 2

Canola oil spray

2 cups fresh or frozen pearl onions

2 large potatoes, halved lengthwise and cut into $1/2$-inch slices

Sea salt and freshly ground black pepper

$1/2$ to $3/4$ pound boneless chuck roast

3 tablespoons tomato paste

$1/3$ cup broth, preferably beef

1 tablespoon plus 1 teaspoon Worcestershire sauce

2 large carrots, sliced into coins, or 1 cup whole baby carrots

2 cups fresh or frozen cut green beans

4 to 6 mushrooms, thickly sliced

CALORIES 663 • PROTEIN 36G • CARBOHYDRATES 55G • FAT 32G • CHOLESTEROL 117MG • SODIUM 302MG • FIBER 9G

Preheat the oven to 450°F.

Spray the inside and lid of a cast-iron Dutch oven with canola oil.

Peel the onions, if using fresh, and drop them into the pot with the potatoes. Mix and lightly season with salt and pepper. Add the meat and again season with salt and pepper.

In a small bowl, whisk together the tomato paste, broth, and Worcestershire sauce until fully incorporated. Pour half of the mixture over the meat.

Add layers of carrots, green beans, and mushrooms and pour in the rest of the sauce.

Cover and bake for 48 minutes for medium/well-done meat and crunchy vegetables, 53 minutes for more well-done meat and softer vegetables, or until the aroma of a fully cooked meal escapes the oven. Serve immediately.

VARIATIONS

Rub the meat with crushed red pepper flakes and white pepper before arranging it in the pot.

Add 1 tablespoon prepared horseradish and 1 tablespoon Dijon mustard to the broth mixture.

Omit the Worcestershire sauce and instead add $^1/_2$ teaspoon each of dried marjoram and dried thyme.

Leave out the entire broth mixture and instead place 3 or 4 sprigs of fresh rosemary in the pot. Be sure to remove the sprigs before serving.

Amaranth Chili

The Aztecs worshipped the life-sustaining properties of amaranth in pre-Columbian times. Sadly, it all but disappeared after the arrival of the conquistadors. A grain (like wheat), amaranth is high in protein, fiber, and amino acids. In this recipe you'll notice the silky beads add yet another exciting texture to this one-pot meal. I find amaranth in the bulk bins at the health food store.

My food processor has a shredding disk, which works well for zucchini; however, sometimes I simply use my grating tower to get the same effect. The shredded zucchini gives this Glorious One-Pot Meal a thick, stewlike consistency that seems especially hearty.

Feel free to swap the amaranth for the same amount of rice (the amount of liquid won't change).

SERVES 2

Olive oil spray
1/4 large onion, chopped
3/4 cup amaranth
3/4 cup broth (beef, chicken, or vegetable) or water
One 15-ounce can black beans, drained and rinsed
1/2 to 3/4 pound ground meat (beef, turkey, or meat-substitute crumbles)

One 4-ounce can diced green chiles, drained
1/2 teaspoon sea salt
1/2 teaspoon ground cumin
1/2 teaspoon dried oregano
2 cups shredded zucchini
3 medium tomatoes, chopped, or one 14-ounce can diced tomatoes, drained

CALORIES 882 • PROTEIN 57G • CARBOHYDRATES 105G • FAT 27G • CHOLESTEROL 99MG • SODIUM 102MG • FIBER 28G

Preheat the oven to 450°F.

Spray the inside and lid of a cast-iron Dutch oven with olive oil.

Scatter the onion in the pot.

Add the amaranth and the liquid. Stir to make an even layer of the grains.

In a medium bowl, mix the beans, meat, chiles, most of the sea salt, the cumin, and the oregano. Drop forkfuls of the mixture into the pot to cover the amaranth.

Top with the zucchini, then the tomatoes. Lightly season with the remaining sea salt.

Cover and bake for 45 minutes, or until 3 minutes after the aroma of a fully cooked meal escapes the oven. Serve immediately.

Beef with Sherried Mushroom Sauce

Barley is a comfort food in my book. Hulled barley is a whole grain and offers all of the health benefits of other whole grains, including cholesterol-lowering qualities and fiber. Use a variety of mushrooms for a deeper, earthier flavor. This recipe tastes great with turkey, too!

I cut and seed winter squash, but often I don't peel it as the peel comes off very easily after it is cooked. You can also make this dish with yellow summer squash. SERVES 2

Olive oil spray

$1/2$ medium onion, thinly sliced

$1/3$ cup sherry

$1/3$ cup broth (preferably beef)

$1/3$ cup milk or milk substitute (soy, rice, or almond milk)

$1/2$ teaspoon freshly ground black pepper

$1/4$ cup hulled barley

$1/2$ to $3/4$ pound beef tenderloin or beef tips

6 ounces mushrooms, sliced (about 2 cups)

$1/2$ acorn or butternut squash, cubed (about 2 cups)

$1/2$ head broccoli, cut into florets, or about 2 cups frozen

CALORIES 616 • PROTEIN 25G • CARBOHYDRATES 32G • FAT 2G • CHOLESTEROL 54MG • SODIUM 114MG • FIBER 127G

Preheat the oven to 450°F.

Spray the inside and lid of a cast-iron Dutch oven with olive oil.

Scatter the onion in the pot.

In a small bowl, whisk together the sherry, broth, milk, and pepper.

Pour the barley into the pot and add about half of the sherry mixture. Stir to make an even layer of the grains.

Add the meat, distribute the mushrooms on top, and pour the rest of the sherry mixture over the meat.

Layer the squash over the meat, then fill the pot with the broccoli.

Cover and bake for 45 minutes, or until 3 minutes after the aroma of a fully cooked meal escapes the oven. Serve immediately.

Corned Beef and Cabbage

Corned beef and cabbage is a meal traditionally eaten by Irish Americans in celebration of St. Patrick's Day in March. Corned *refers* to the large salt crystals (corns) rubbed into the meat to preserve it. The corned beef has enough spices to flavor this recipe, but if you feel the need for more spice, include the sea salt and pepper. For more gravy, simply add more broth to the recipe.

I use lunch-meat-style corned beef in a thick slice from the deli in this recipe simply because it's hard to find a package of raw, seasoned corned beef that's less than two pounds. However, you can certainly use raw corned beef if you prefer. SERVES 2

Canola oil spray

1 medium onion, halved and thinly sliced

1 celery stalk, thinly sliced

$1/2$ to $3/4$ pound corned beef from the deli

1 large russet potato, unpeeled and cut into $1/2$-inch cubes

1 cup sliced carrots

$1/2$ head green cabbage, roughly chopped (about 4 cups)

$1/4$ cup broth (beef, chicken, or vegetable)

$1/8$ teaspoon allspice

$1/8$ teaspoon sea salt, optional

$1/8$ teaspoon freshly ground black pepper, optional

1 bay leaf

Preheat the oven to 450°F.

Spray the inside and lid of a cast-iron Dutch oven with canola oil.

Separate the onion slices into half rings and scatter in the pot along with the celery.

Add the corned beef, then layer the potatoes and carrots. Pack in as much cabbage as possible to fill the pot.

In a measuring cup, mix the broth, allspice, and salt and pepper, if desired, until there are no clumps of spices. Pour the mixture over the cabbage and add the bay leaf.

Cover tightly and bake for about 30 minutes, or until 3 minutes after the aroma of a fully cooked meal escapes the oven. Serve immediately. Discard the bay leaf and spoon the juices at the bottom of the pot over each serving.

Argentinian Beef

Feel free to make this recipe using ground turkey or pork instead of beef, or even meat-substitute crumbles. You could also use a tenderloin cut of meat. Look for peeled and chopped butternut squash in your supermarket vegetable aisle. SERVES 2

Olive oil spray

$^1/_2$ medium onion, minced

$^1/_2$ red bell pepper, cored, seeded, and minced

8 to 10 cremini mushrooms, sliced

$^1/_2$ teaspoon ground cumin

Sea salt and freshly ground black pepper

$^1/_2$ to $^3/_4$ pound ground meat

1 cup white rice

1 cup plus 1 tablespoon broth (preferably beef) or water

2 cups peeled, cubed butternut squash

$^1/_2$ head broccoli, cut into florets (about 2 cups)

Preheat the oven to 450°F.

Spray the inside and lid of a cast-iron Dutch oven with olive oil.

In a large bowl, mix the onion, bell pepper, mushrooms, cumin, salt, and pepper. Add the meat to the bowl and mix well. Set aside. If using tenderloins rather than ground meat, set the onion-spice mixture aside and simply spoon over the steaks in step 5.

Rinse the rice in a strainer until the water runs clear. Tip the rice into the pot, add the liquid, and stir to make an even layer.

Drop ragged forkfuls of the meat mixture into the pot. If using tenderloins, arrange them in the pot and blanket with the onion-spice mixture.

Arrange the squash in a layer, then load in the broccoli until the pot is full.

Cover and bake for about 45 minutes, or until 3 minutes after the aroma of a fully cooked meal escapes the oven. Serve immediately.

CALORIES 701 • PROTEIN 39G • CARBOHYDRATES 94G • FAT 24G • CHOLESTEROL 99MG • SODIUM 119MG • FIBER 8G

Dinner for Dad

· ·

The concept of this meal is that it is so easy and safe (no knife work) that a child could prepare it as a Father's Day treat. Of course, the recipe is easily doubled or tripled. What may surprise you is how delicious it is! Feel free to use your favorite steak sauce, teriyaki sauce, barbecue sauce, or Worcestershire sauce. If your dad doesn't like steak, feel free to substitute any other protein (chicken, fish, pork, etc.).

The steak should turn out well done on the edges and medium rare in the center. For more fully cooked meat, bake for at least 30 minutes. SERVES 2

Canola oil spray

10 to 12 ounces frozen hash browns (not the patties)

Sea salt

2 cups frozen pearl onions

$^1/_2$ to $^3/_4$ pound boneless steak or tenderloin, well trimmed

2 tablespoons steak sauce (A-1 or other brand)

5 to 10 mushrooms, sliced (about 1 cup)

$1^1/_2$ cups whole baby carrots

$2^1/_2$ cups frozen cut green beans

2 fresh rosemary sprigs

Preheat the oven to 450°F.

Spray the inside and lid of a cast-iron Dutch oven with canola oil.

Shake the hash browns into the pot to distribute evenly and season lightly with salt. Scatter the onions over the potatoes; then add the steak. Spread steak sauce on the meat and scatter in the mushrooms.

Distribute the carrots in a layer and then fill the pot with green beans. Tuck the rosemary sprigs into crevices.

Cover and bake for about 30 minutes, or until 3 minutes after the aroma of a fully cooked meal escapes the oven. Serve immediately.

CALORIES 500 • PROTEIN 37G • CARBOHYDRATES 42G • FAT 19G • CHOLESTEROL 102MG • SODIUM 365MG • FIBER 11G

Fiesta Steak

If your steak is very thick, you may need to add up to eight minutes more in the oven. Let your nose be your guide.

This recipe is chock full of vegetables—a great way to get your meat lover to eat vegetables, too! Try this recipe with chicken pieces instead of steak for a change.

My aunt swears by kosher salt and freshly squeezed lemon or lime when cooking meat, but I prefer to use sea salt whenever I'm cooking. SERVES 2

Olive oil spray

1 cup white rice

1 cup plus 1 tablespoon broth (beef or vegetable) or water

$^{1}/_{4}$ cup freshly squeezed lime juice (2 to 3 limes)

1 tablespoon chopped fresh cilantro

1 tablespoon chopped fresh oregano

1 teaspoon ground cumin

$^{1}/_{2}$ to $^{3}/_{4}$ pound boneless steak

Sea salt and freshly cracked black pepper

4 garlic cloves, chopped

$^{1}/_{2}$ onion, halved and thinly sliced

$^{1}/_{2}$ yellow bell pepper, cored, seeded, and sliced into strips

$^{1}/_{2}$ red bell pepper, cored, seeded, and sliced into strips

$^{1}/_{2}$ green bell pepper, cored, seeded, and sliced into strips

CALORIES 611 • PROTEIN 39G • CARBOHYDRATES 81G • FAT 17G • CHOLESTEROL 81MG • SODIUM 87MG • FIBER 4G

Preheat the oven to 450°F.

Spray the inside and lid of a cast-iron Dutch oven with olive oil.

Rinse the rice in a strainer under cold water until the water runs clear. Tip the rice into the pot, add the liquid, and stir to make an even layer.

In a small bowl, stir together the lime juice, cilantro, oregano, and cumin.

Add the steak to the pot, season with salt and pepper, and spoon half of the lime juice mixture over the meat.

Sprinkle the garlic over the steak and top with the onion. Then scatter on the bell pepper strips, and spoon the rest of the lime juice mixture over all.

Cover and bake for 45 minutes, or until 3 minutes after the aroma of a fully cooked meal escapes the oven. Serve immediately.

Flageolets and Sausage

Sausage and beans make a hearty winter meal. If you don't have fresh tomatoes on hand, use a drained 14-ounce can of diced tomatoes instead. If you don't have flageolets, other beans to try include Great Northern and cannellini beans.

To make this a lower-fat dinner, use turkey or chicken sausage instead of pork. Health food stores typically have many types of sausages available at the meat counter. Experiment with flavors such as applewood-smoked sausage, habañero chile, or spicy Italian. SERVES 2

Olive oil spray

$^1/_2$ onion, halved and thinly sliced

3 garlic cloves, chopped

One 14-ounce can flageolets, Great Northern beans, or cannellini beans

1 teaspoon dried thyme, or 1 tablespoon chopped fresh

$^1/_2$ teaspoon celery seeds

Sea salt and freshly ground black pepper

2 or 3 large sausage links ($^1/_2$ to $^3/_4$ pound)

1 small zucchini, thinly sliced

3 medium tomatoes, chopped

Preheat the oven to 450°F.

Spray the inside and lid of a cast-iron Dutch oven with olive oil.

Scatter the onion and garlic in the pot.

Drain and rinse the beans and add to the pot, making a smooth layer. Sprinkle with the thyme and celery seeds and season with salt and pepper.

Place the sausage on the beans. Toss in the zucchini, top with the tomatoes, and again, season with salt and pepper.

Cover and bake for 35 minutes, or until 3 minutes after the aroma of a fully cooked meal escapes the oven. Serve immediately.

CALORIES 373 • PROTEIN 24G • CARBOHYDRATES 29G • FAT 19G • CHOLESTEROL 40G • SODIUM 875MG • FIBER 9G

Honey and Spice Pork

My kids love the sweet and spicy flavors of this meal. The pork together with the potatoes, carrots, and green beans offers a kid-friendly, well-rounded dinner loaded with nutrients and low in fat. Look for boneless center-cut pork loin, 1/2 inch thick. Or substitute a turkey tenderloin, a salmon fillet, or even chicken for the pork. SERVES 2

Canola oil spray
1/2 to 3/4 pound pork tenderloin
Sea salt and freshly ground black pepper
1/4 cup honey
3 tablespoons Dijon or Cajun-style mustard
1/2 teaspoon ground ginger

1/2 teaspoon ground cinnamon
1/4 teaspoon ground cloves
6 to 8 small new potatoes
2 carrots, sliced into coins
2 cups fresh or frozen cut green beans

Preheat the oven to 450°F.

Spray the inside and lid of a cast-iron Dutch oven with canola oil.

Put the pork in the pot and lightly season with salt and pepper.

In a small bowl, mix the honey, mustard, ginger, cinnamon, and cloves and pour over the pork.

Slice the potatoes in half and add to the pot, then scatter the carrots and green beans over the potatoes.

Cover and bake for 45 minutes, or until 3 minutes after the aroma of a fully cooked meal escapes the oven. Serve immediately.

CALORIES 507 • PROTEIN 41G • CARBOHYDRATES 79G • FAT 6G • CHOLESTEROL 105MG • SODIUM 475MG • FIBER 7G

Hearty Polenta and Sausage

Turkey sausage—especially the hot and spicy kind—is excellent in this dish. Wild mushrooms add a hearty flavor that complements the sausage, but common white mushrooms do just fine here as well. To use dried mushrooms, place in a bowl, cover with boiling water, and steep while you prepare the rest of the ingredients (ten to twenty minutes). When softened, drain well and slice.

If using frozen spinach, try to break the block into a few pieces to spread around in the pot. If it is simply too hard to break, don't worry. It will still cook fine, although you may find you need to cook the meal another five to ten minutes for the polenta to soften completely. As always with these recipes, use your nose as your guide. SERVES 2

Olive oil spray

$^1/_2$ cup dry polenta

$1^1/_2$ cups broth (beef, chicken, or vegetable) or water

4 to 8 garlic cloves, minced

1 teaspoon dried basil, or 1 tablespoon chopped fresh

2 or 3 spicy sausages, fresh or frozen ($^1/_2$ to $^3/_4$ pound)

4 to 8 mushrooms, sliced

$^1/_2$ yellow bell pepper, cored, seeded, and sliced into strips

1 carrot, sliced into coins

Sea salt and freshly ground black pepper

One 10-ounce package frozen spinach, or 2 large handfuls fresh

3 tablespoons grated Parmesan cheese, optional

CALORIES 414 • PROTEIN 23G • CARBOHYDRATES 34G • FAT 21G • CHOLESTEROL 47MG • SODIUM 689MG • FIBER 2G

Preheat the oven to 450°F.

Spray the inside and lid of a cast-iron Dutch oven with olive oil.

Pour the polenta in the bottom of the pot and add the liquid. Stir to smooth the grains into an even layer, then sprinkle in a large pinch of the garlic and basil.

Add the sausages, followed by the mushrooms, bell pepper, and carrot.

Sprinkle another large pinch of garlic and basil and season lightly with salt and pepper.

Add the spinach and the rest of the garlic and basil.

Cover and bake for 45 minutes, or until 3 minutes after the aroma of a fully cooked meal escapes the oven. Serve immediately with grated Parmesan, if desired.

Indian Almond Curry Lamb

This is a variation of a traditional Indian curried lamb dish called roghan josh. *Typically this dish calls for mixing heavy whipping cream into the tomato sauce, but this version retains all the taste without the extra saturated fat. If you want, add two tablespoons of heavy whipping cream or milk to the tomato sauce and cook as directed.*

Turkey tenderloin or beef stew chunks make wonderful substitutions for the lamb in this recipe. The lentils can be omitted entirely, or you can use couscous instead (see the chart on page 8 for recommended couscous and liquid amounts). The lentils in this recipe will emerge al dente; for softer lentils, use canned and omit the half cup of water. SERVES 2

Olive oil spray
1/4 cup green lentils
1/4 medium red onion, halved and thinly sliced
1/4 teaspoon cumin seeds
1 tablespoon grated fresh ginger
3 to 5 garlic cloves, chopped
Sea salt and freshly ground black pepper
1/4 cup slivered almonds
1/8 teaspoon ground cardamom

1/8 teaspoon ground coriander
1/8 teaspoon cayenne
1/8 teaspoon ground cloves
1/2 to 3/4 pound boneless leg of lamb, trimmed well and cut into 2-inch cubes
1/2 green bell pepper, cored, seeded, and thinly sliced
1 tablespoon chopped fresh cilantro
1/2 cup canned tomato sauce

CALORIES 464 • PROTEIN 49G • CARBOHYDRATES 23G • FAT 19G • CHOLESTEROL 122MG • SODIUM 370MG • FIBER 7G

Preheat the oven to 450°F.

Spray the inside and lid of a cast-iron Dutch oven with olive oil.

Rinse the lentils in a mesh strainer and pour into the pot. Add $^1/_2$ cup boiling water and stir to distribute the lentils in an even layer.

Scatter the onion over the lentils. Sprinkle on the cumin, ginger, and garlic and lightly season with salt and pepper.

In a medium bowl, combine the almonds, cardamom, coriander, cayenne, cloves, and black pepper to taste. Add the meat and stir to coat, then add the mixture in forkfuls to the pot, making an uneven layer. Cover with the bell pepper. Stir the cilantro into the tomato sauce and pour the mixture over the top.

Cover and bake for 45 minutes, or until 3 minutes after the aroma of a fully cooked meal escapes the oven. Serve immediately.

Lemon Lamb

Summer is tomato time; be sure to try the new heirloom varieties. In winter, I usually find that Roma, or plum, tomatoes are the most flavorful. Oil-cured olives will add other notes, but use water-packed olives if you're looking to cut back on fat.

Make a quick broth with part of a bouillon cube. Purchase bouillon from health food stores for versions lower in sodium and other preservatives.

An easy way to trim exactly the right amount from the bottom of an asparagus stalk is simply to grab an end in each hand and bend until it snaps. It will break at the point where the stalk becomes less woody. SERVES 2

Olive oil spray

1 shallot, or $^1/_2$ small yellow onion, chopped

$^1/_2$ cup couscous

$^1/_2$ cup broth (preferably beef) or water

$^1/_2$ to $^3/_4$ pound boneless lamb, cubed

Sea salt and freshly ground black pepper

$^1/_2$ teaspoon dried oregano

1 tablespoon chopped fresh parsley

2 or 3 garlic cloves, chopped

2 teaspoons grated lemon zest

$^1/_2$ cup pitted olives, halved

2 medium tomatoes, sliced $^3/_4$ inch thick

10 to 15 asparagus stalks, trimmed, or 2 handfuls spinach, roughly chopped

CALORIES 908 • PROTEIN 86G • CARBOHYDRATES 57G • FAT 244G • CHOLESTEROL 244MG • SODIUM 138MG • FIBER 6G

Preheat the oven to 450°F.

Spray the inside and lid of a cast-iron Dutch oven with olive oil.

Scatter the shallot in the pot. Pour in the couscous and add the broth. Stir to make an even layer.

Put the lamb on the couscous and lightly season with salt and pepper. Sprinkle with the oregano, parsley, garlic, and lemon zest. Add a layer of olives.

Lay the tomatoes on top followed by the asparagus.

Cover and bake for about 45 minutes, or until 3 minutes after the aroma of a fully cooked meal escapes the oven. Serve immediately.

Mediterranean Steak

For me, this flavor is reminiscent of the south of France, along the Côte d'Azur with its crystalline blue waters. Of course, fresh herbs would be fantastic here if you have them. If using fresh herbs, use one tablespoon of each. SERVES 2

Olive oil spray

4 to 6 garlic cloves, chopped

1/2 cup whole wheat couscous

1/2 cup broth (beef or vegetable) or water

1/2 to 3/4 pound boneless beef tenderloin, trimmed well

1/4 cup red wine

1 tablespoon olive oil

1 tablespoon fresh lemon juice

1/2 teaspoon dried marjoram

1/2 teaspoon dried thyme

2 cups fresh or frozen pearl onions

4 plum tomatoes, quartered

1/2 head broccoli, cut into florets (about 2 cups)

Preheat the oven to 450°F.

Spray the inside and lid of a cast-iron Dutch oven with olive oil.

Scatter half the garlic in the pot. Pour in the couscous and liquid. Stir to distribute the couscous in an even layer. Add the steak and sprinkle with the rest of the garlic.

In a small bowl, mix the wine, olive oil, lemon juice, marjoram, and thyme. Pour half of the mixture over the steak. Drop in the onions and arrange the tomato quarters skin side down.

Fill the rest of the pot with broccoli and pour the remaining wine mixture over all.

Cover and bake for 45 minutes, or until 3 minutes after the aroma of a fully cooked meal escapes the oven. Serve immediately.

CALORIES 724 • PROTEIN 40G • CARBOHYDRATES 60G • FAT 34G • CHOLESTEROL 98MG • SODIUM 144MG • FIBER 11G

Pasta with Meatballs

I always keep jars of organic marinara sauce in my pantry for convenient Glorious One-Pot Meal options, including this easy version of pasta with meatballs.

Use whatever type of ground meat you prefer: beef, pork, turkey, chicken, or even soy or other meat substitutes. Make a quantity of meatballs in advance and freeze them individually on cookie sheets. Then drop the frozen balls into a plastic storage container and keep in the freezer for spur-of-the-moment Glorious One-Pot Meals. SERVES 2

Olive oil spray
2 cups rotini or fusilli
$1/2$ teaspoon olive oil
$1/2$ to $3/4$ pound ground meat
1 large egg, lightly beaten
$1/4$ cup bread crumbs
$1/4$ teaspoon sea salt

2 tablespoons chopped fresh parsley
One 12-ounce jar marinara sauce
2 carrots, sliced into coins
$1/2$ medium zucchini, halved lengthwise and cut into $1/2$-inch slices
$1/2$ yellow bell pepper, cored, seeded, and sliced

Preheat the oven to 450°F.

Spray the inside and lid of a cast-iron Dutch oven with olive oil.

Scatter the pasta in the pot. Add $2/3$ cup water and olive oil and stir to make an even layer.

In a medium bowl, mix the ground meat with the egg, bread crumbs, salt, and parsley. Shape the mixture into balls, about 2 tablespoons each, and drop into the pot. Cover with half of the marinara sauce.

Layer in the carrots, zucchini, and bell pepper; then lightly season with salt. Pour the rest of the marinara sauce over all.

Cover and bake for about 45 minutes, or until 3 minutes after the aroma of a fully cooked meal escapes the oven. Serve immediately.

CALORIES 724 • PROTEIN 45G • CARBOHYDRATES 74G • FAT 28G • CHOLESTEROL 206MG • SODIUM 133MG • FIBER 8G

Pasta Tricolore

All of the ingredients in this festive meal can be found in your pantry or freezer, making it a convenient wintertime treat. However, try to break up a frozen block of ground meat before adding it to the pot.

There's no need to defrost a package of frozen spinach. Let it sit on the counter to soften while preparing other ingredients. Cut it into chunks using a sharp knife, then stir the chunks into the meat mixture. Fresh spinach can be chopped slightly and mixed with the meat, or kept whole and layered on top. SERVES 2

Olive oil spray
2 cups pasta (penne, farfalle, etc.)
One 14-ounce can tomatoes
1 to 4 garlic cloves, minced
Sea salt and freshly ground black pepper
$^1/_2$ teaspoon olive oil

$^1/_4$ medium onion, chopped
1 tablespoon chopped fresh basil
1 tablespoon chopped fresh oregano
One 10-ounce package frozen spinach, or
  2 large handfuls fresh
$^1/_2$ to $^3/_4$ pound ground beef or turkey

CALORIES 425 • PROTEIN 21G • CARBOHYDRATES 51G • FAT 14G • CHOLESTEROL 43MG • SODIUM 512MG • FIBER 5G

Preheat the oven to 450°F.

Spray the inside and lid of a cast-iron Dutch oven with olive oil.

Scatter the pasta in the pot.

Drain the liquid from the tomatoes into a measuring cup. If necessary, add enough water to make $2/3$ cup liquid. Reserve the tomatoes.

Add one-third of the garlic, a little salt and pepper, and the olive oil to the tomato liquid. Pour the liquid into the pot and stir to make the pasta an even layer.

Mix the tomatoes with the rest of the garlic, the onion, basil and oregano, spinach, and ground meat in a medium bowl. Season with salt and pepper to taste.

Drop forkfuls of the tomato-meat mixture evenly over the pasta without mixing together.

Cover and bake for 45 minutes, or until 3 minutes after the aroma of a fully cooked meal escapes the oven. Serve immediately.

Sausage and Quinoa

Quinoa (pronounced KEEN-wah) has a light, nutty flavor with a wonderful texture that makes it fun to eat. Quinoa is the only grain that is a complete protein. It was the staple food of the Incas in Peru, who called it "the Mother grain." Find it near the rice or in the bulk food section of a health food store or your grocer's natural foods aisle. Store it in an airtight jar.

Use your family's favorite type of sausage to make this recipe a real winner. Our current favorite is an organic chicken-feta sausage that we find in our regular grocer's freezer. There is no need to thaw frozen sausages; just be sure to separate them before adding them to the Dutch oven.

Try this recipe with toasted buckwheat groats, also called kasha, for a change in flavor. SERVES 2

Olive oil spray
$^3/_4$ cup quinoa
1 cup broth (chicken or vegetable) or water
$^1/_2$ to $^3/_4$ pound sausage links
$^1/_2$ green bell pepper, cored, seeded, and sliced

$^1/_2$ yellow bell pepper, cored, seeded, and sliced
$^1/_2$ red bell pepper, cored, seeded, and sliced
Sea salt
4 plum tomatoes, quartered lengthwise

Preheat the oven to 450°F.

Spray the inside and lid of a cast-iron Dutch oven with olive oil.

Pour the quinoa into the pot, add the liquid, and stir to coat the grains and make an even layer.

Add the sausages to the pot in a single layer, if possible. Scatter the bell peppers on top and lightly season with salt. Top with the tomato wedges.

Cover and bake for about 45 minutes, or until 3 minutes after the aroma of a fully cooked meal escapes the oven. Fluff the quinoa with a fork when serving. Serve immediately.

CALORIES 531 • PROTEIN 28G • CARBOHYDRATES 57G • FAT 22G • CHOLESTEROL 40MG • SODIUM 562MG • FIBER 7G

Southwestern Quinoa

Quinoa is not only a complete protein, providing all the essential amino acids, it's also gluten-free. This light and delicate grain has a delicious nutty flavor that is perfect for summer weather.

The type of chile is up to you. For a milder flavor, choose an Anaheim green chile; pasillas or jalapeños will give more of a bite.

You may use spinach rather than kale or chard. If you find that your greens emerge browner than you'd like, move them down a layer and top with the bell pepper instead. SERVES 2

Olive oil spray

³/4 cup quinoa

1 cup broth (chicken or vegetable) or water

¹/2 teaspoon ground cumin

¹/2 to ³/4 pound beef or turkey, tenderloin or ground

¹/8 teaspoon sea salt

1 scallion, white and green parts, sliced

1 green chile, stemmed, seeded, and chopped

1 small summer squash, halved lengthwise and sliced into 1-inch pieces

¹/2 red bell pepper, cored, seeded, and sliced

3 or 4 kale or Swiss chard leaves, stemmed and roughly chopped (about 2 cups)

¹/2 cup salsa, optional

Preheat the oven to 450°F.

Spray the inside and lid of a cast-iron Dutch oven with olive oil.

Pour in the quinoa. Add the liquid and cumin and stir to dissolve the cumin and evenly coat the grains. Add the meat and sprinkle with the salt, scallion, and chile.

Add the squash in a layer, followed by the bell pepper.

Top with the greens, making certain none hangs over the edge. If using, pour the salsa over all.

Cover and bake for about 35 minutes, or until 3 minutes after the aroma of a fully cooked meal escapes the oven. Serve immediately.

CALORIES 402 • PROTEIN 14G • CARBOHYDRATES 56G • FAT 11G • CHOLESTEROL 86MG • SODIUM 268MG • FIBER 7G

Sun-Dried Tomato Lamb

For rarer meat, chop the potatoes, carrots, and cauliflower into smaller pieces, as they will cook more quickly that way and become tender before the meat is cooked through. Try this recipe with steak tenderloin or a turkey tenderloin if you don't want lamb.

Use boneless lamb fillets in this meal as bones just take up precious real estate in your pot. Trim the meat well of fat.

Sun-dried tomatoes come either packed in oil or dry. Either is fine to use here. SERVES 2

Olive oil spray

$^1/_2$ to $^3/_4$ pound boneless lamb fillets, trimmed well

3 sun-dried tomatoes, minced

2 garlic cloves, chopped

1 russet potato, unpeeled and cubed

2 carrots, sliced into coins

Sea salt

1 tablespoon honey

1 tablespoon fresh lemon juice

1 tablespoon chopped fresh parsley

$^1/_2$ teaspoon ground cumin

2 cups bite-size cauliflower florets

2 cups fresh or frozen cut green beans

CALORIES 474 • PROTEIN 37G • CARBOHYDRATES 42G • FAT 19G • CHOLESTEROL 116MG • SODIUM 123MG • FIBER 10G

Preheat the oven to 450°F.

Spray the inside and lid of a cast-iron Dutch oven with olive oil.

Put the lamb in the pot.

Combine the tomatoes and garlic, then spread over the lamb.

Arrange the potato and carrots around the meat and lightly season with salt.

In a small bowl, mix the honey, lemon juice, parsley, and cumin. Pour half the mixture over the carrots and potato, then add the cauliflower.

Fill the rest of the pot with the green beans and then pour the remaining honey mixture over all.

Cover and bake for about 40 minutes, or until 3 minutes after the aroma of a fully cooked meal escapes the oven. Serve immediately.

Thai Larb

Larb is traditional Thai comfort food. The mint adds a clean jolt of flavor to this casserole-type meal. My cousin Abi lived in Thailand for a time and helped me fine-tune my version of this classic dish. Typically, the meat and rice are served over raw cabbage, but we think this style is pretty tasty as well. You can use serrano, Anaheim, or almost any other kind of chile pepper if you can't find a jalapeño. Of course, your meal will be as spicy as your chile. Consider adding 1 tablespoon of chopped fresh basil or cilantro to the mint mixture for a slightly different taste. SERVES 2

Canola oil spray

1 cup jasmine rice

1 cup broth (beef, chicken, or vegetable) or water

Grated zest of 1 lime (about 1 tablespoon)

Grated zest of 1 lemon (about 1 tablespoon)

$^1/_4$ cup fresh lime juice

1 tablespoon fresh lemon juice

1 tablespoon fish sauce or soy sauce

1 tablespoon rice vinegar

$1^1/_2$ teaspoons light brown sugar

1 teaspoon minced jalapeño chile

$^1/_8$ teaspoon red pepper flakes

2 scallions, white and green parts, chopped

$^1/_2$ red or orange bell pepper, cored, seeded, and diced

$^1/_4$ cup chopped fresh mint

$^1/_2$ to $^3/_4$ pound ground meat (beef, poultry, or pork)

$^1/_4$ head green cabbage, chopped (about 2 cups)

1 cup snow peas

CALORIES 652 • PROTEIN 35G • CARBOHYDRATES 81G • FAT 21G • CHOLESTEROL 99MG • SODIUM 123MG • FIBER 4G

Preheat the oven to 450°F.

Spray the inside and lid of a cast-iron Dutch oven with canola oil.

Rinse the rice in a strainer under cold water until the water runs clear. Tip the rice into the pot, add the liquid, and stir to make an even layer.

In a medium bowl, combine the lime and lemon zest, lime and lemon juice, fish sauce, rice vinegar, brown sugar, jalapeño, red pepper flakes, scallions, bell pepper, and mint. Whisk until the sugar dissolves. Add the meat to the mixture and stir with a fork to break up the meat and incorporate the mint mixture throughout.

Drop forkfuls of the meat mixture into the pot, arranging them evenly but without packing them together.

Add a thick layer of cabbage and top with the snow peas.

Cover and bake for 45 minutes, or until 3 minutes after the aroma of a fully cooked meal escapes the oven. Serve immediately.

POULTRY

African Peanut Butter Stew

Once, when I was visiting Paris, my friend Emile from Gabon, Africa, made this dish for me. I was amazed that cooking with peanut butter could be so good. SERVES 2

Canola oil spray or 2 teaspoons peanut oil

1/2 medium onion, diced

3/4 cup white rice

3/4 cup plus 1 tablespoon broth (chicken or vegetable) or water

1/2 to 3/4 pound chicken breasts or thighs

1/2 red bell pepper, cored, seeded, and sliced

2/3 cup milk (skim is okay) or water

2 to 4 garlic cloves, minced or crushed

1/2 teaspoon cayenne

Sea salt

3 tablespoons peanut butter, creamy or chunky

3 or 4 tomatoes, diced, or one 14-ounce can diced, drained

1/2 sweet potato, cut into 3/4-inch cubes

1 handful fresh spinach, or about 5 ounces frozen

CALORIES 426 • PROTEIN 27G • CARBOHYDRATES 33G • FAT 15G • CHOLESTEROL 39MG • SODIUM 626MG • FIBER 9G

Preheat the oven to 450°F.

Spray the inside and lid of a cast-iron Dutch oven with canola oil or wipe with peanut oil.

Scatter the onion in the pot.

Rinse the rice in a strainer under cold water until the water runs clear. Tip the rice into the pot, add the liquid, and stir to make an even layer.

Place the chicken on the rice. Add the bell pepper.

In a measuring cup, whisk the milk, garlic, cayenne, salt, and peanut butter until the peanut butter dissolves. Pour over the chicken.

Layer in the tomatoes, sweet potato, and spinach.

Cover and bake for 45 minutes, or until 3 minutes after the aroma of a fully cooked meal escapes the oven. Serve immediately.

VARIATIONS

Use coconut milk instead of milk. Substituting soy or rice milk is also always acceptable in a Glorious One-Pot Meal.

Substitute a minced jalapeño chile instead of the cayenne. Or use four shakes of red pepper flakes.

Shrimp and/or scallops instead of, or along with, the chicken taste great, too. Or try tofu (use extra-firm cubes).

Use sweet or white potatoes instead of rice.

Bahamian Chicken

The spicy tropical tastes of the Bahamas can be yours without leaving home! As in all the recipes, there's no need to peel the potatoes; in fact, the skin is the most nutritious part, so save yourself the trouble and leave it on. And try this meal with sweet potatoes rather than white, or substitute pork for the chicken. Use seitan (a wheat product found near the tofu in the refrigerated section of your health food store) for a vegetarian alternative. SERVES 2

Canola oil spray

$1/2$ teaspoon cumin seeds

$1/2$ to $3/4$ pound chicken breasts or thighs

Sea salt and freshly ground black pepper

2 to 4 garlic cloves, chopped

1 medium potato, cut into 1-inch cubes

$1/2$ red or orange bell pepper, cored, seeded, and cut into 1-inch wedges

$1/2$ small yellow summer squash, cut into 1-inch chunks

$1/2$ head broccoli, cut into florets (about 2 cups)

3 tablespoons rice or wine vinegar

3 tablespoons fresh orange juice

$1/2$ teaspoon dried oregano

$1/2$ teaspoon paprika

$1/4$ teaspoon ground allspice

$1/4$ teaspoon red pepper flakes

CALORIES 210 • PROTEIN 29G • CARBOHYDRATES 18G • FAT 4G • CHOLESTEROL 75MG • SODIUM 590MG • FIBER 3G

Preheat the oven to 450°F.

Spray the inside and lid of a cast-iron Dutch oven with canola oil.

Sprinkle the cumin seeds in the pot. Place the chicken in the pot and lightly season with salt and pepper; sprinkle with the garlic.

Arrange the potato on top of the chicken. Add the bell pepper, squash, and broccoli in layers.

In a small bowl, mix the vinegar, orange juice, oregano, paprika, allspice, black pepper to taste, and red pepper flakes. Pour over the vegetables.

Cover and bake for 45 minutes, or until 3 minutes after the aroma of a fully cooked meal escapes the oven. Serve immediately.

California Chicken

In a pinch, substitute a drained can of diced tomatoes for fresh and any kind of wine for the dry sherry. For light and fluffy couscous, fluff it with a fork and let sit for a few minutes before eating.

An easy way to peel an avocado is to halve it lengthwise and remove the pit by striking it firmly with the blade of a knife and twisting slightly to loosen. Then, make a few lengthwise cuts and a few cuts across, making sure not to pierce the skin. Push the avocado inside out and effortlessly knock the cubes of flesh from the skin. SERVES 2

Olive or canola oil spray

$^1/_2$ cup couscous

$^1/_2$ to $^3/_4$ pound chicken breasts or thighs

$^1/_4$ teaspoon freshly ground black pepper

$^1/_2$ green bell pepper, cored, seeded, and cut into strips

2 tomatoes, cut into wedges

$^1/_2$ cup small pitted ripe olives, sliced

1 firm-ripe avocado, sliced or cubed

$^1/_2$ medium onion, chopped

1 teaspoon celery salt

$^1/_4$ teaspoon dried marjoram

$^1/_4$ teaspoon dried basil

1 tablespoon dry sherry

1 tablespoon fresh lemon juice

CALORIES 566 • PROTEIN 36G • CARBOHYDRATES 54G • FAT 24G • CHOLESTEROL 75MG • SODIUM 1015MG • FIBER 11G

Preheat the oven to 450°F.

Spray the inside and lid of a cast-iron Dutch oven with olive or canola oil.

Pour the couscous into the pot. Add $^1/_2$ cup water and stir to make an even layer of the grains.

Arrange the chicken on top of the couscous and season lightly with pepper.

Add the bell pepper, tomatoes, and olives in separate layers, and again season lightly with pepper. Layer the avocado on top of everything.

In a small bowl, combine the onion, celery salt, marjoram, basil, sherry, and lemon juice and distribute over the ingredients in the pot.

Cover and bake for 45 minutes, or until 3 minutes after the aroma of a fully cooked meal escapes the oven. Serve immediately.

Chicken Cacciatore

This is an easy dish, perfect both for chilly nights and for when you have an abundance of vegetables. Cacciatore means "hunter" in Italian. This is the dish hunters would make from whatever was available after a day of hunting and foraging.

Use any vegetables you wish—try cubed eggplant, sliced carrots, green beans, spinach, broccoli, cauliflower florets. Orzo is rice-shaped pasta, but bow ties (farfalle) also work well in this meal.

For a heartier flavor, substitute dry white wine for the water plus part of the tomato liquid, and use chicken on the bone. If using fresh herbs instead of dried, use one tablespoon of each. SERVES 2

Olive oil spray

$^1/_4$ medium onion, thinly sliced

One 14-ounce can tomatoes

$^1/_2$ teaspoon dried basil

$^1/_2$ teaspoon dried oregano

$^1/_2$ teaspoon dried marjoram

1 cup orzo

$^1/_2$ to $^3/_4$ pound chicken breasts or thighs

Sea salt and freshly ground black pepper

3 to 5 garlic cloves, chopped

$^1/_2$ small yellow squash, halved lengthwise and cut into $^1/_2$-inch slices

$^1/_2$ small zucchini, halved lengthwise and cut into $^1/_2$-inch slices

$^1/_2$ green bell pepper, cored, seeded, and julienned

$^1/_2$ red bell pepper, cored, seeded, and julienned

1 tablespoon drained capers, optional

CALORIES 304 • PROTEIN 32G • CARBOHYDRATES 34G • FAT 4G • CHOLESTEROL 75MG • SODIUM 660MG • FIBER 4G

Preheat the oven to 450°F.

Spray the inside and lid of a cast-iron Dutch oven with olive oil.

Scatter the onion in the pot.

Drain the tomatoes into a large measuring cup and add water as needed to make 1 cup of liquid. Mix the tomato liquid with the herbs. Chop the tomatoes and set aside.

Add the orzo to the pot in an even layer. Pour $^3/4$ cup of the herbed liquid over the orzo.

Place the chicken on the orzo and lightly season with salt and pepper. Sprinkle with the garlic.

Spread the tomatoes over the chicken. Layer in the squash, zucchini, and bell peppers, and season lightly with salt and pepper to taste. Pour the remaining $^1/4$ cup of herbed liquid over all. If using, scatter the capers on top.

Cover and bake for 45 minutes, or until 3 minutes after the aroma of a fully cooked meal escapes the oven. Serve immediately.

Chicken Marbella

This was a popular and exotic dinner party recipe in the "mod" 1960s. My mother-in-law made the traditional version for us recently, and though my husband typically doesn't like fruit with meat, even he licked his plate clean! I cut the amount of brown sugar called for in the original version immensely because I feel the prunes add a lot of sweetness. You could even omit the sugar entirely and still enjoy a sweet-tasting meal. SERVES 2

Olive oil spray

1/2 to 3/4 pound chicken breasts or thighs

1/4 cup pitted prunes, chopped

1/4 cup pitted Spanish green olives, halved

2 tablespoons capers, with a bit of juice

2 tablespoons red wine vinegar

2 tablespoons olive oil

1/4 cup white wine

2 tablespoons light brown sugar

2 teaspoons dried oregano

2 teaspoons finely chopped fresh parsley

6 to 8 new potatoes, cubed

Sea salt

2 portobello mushrooms, sliced

8 to 10 Brussels sprouts (about 6 ounces), trimmed and halved lengthwise

2 bay leaves

Preheat the oven to 450°F.

Spray the inside and lid of a cast-iron Dutch oven with olive oil.

Arrange the chicken in a single layer in the pot. Sprinkle with the prunes, olives, and capers.

In a small bowl, mix the vinegar, olive oil, wine, brown sugar, oregano, and parsley until the sugar dissolves. Pour half of the mixture evenly over the chicken. Add the potatoes and season lightly with salt.

Spread the mushrooms in a layer. Top with the Brussels sprouts. Pour the rest of the liquid over all and tuck the bay leaves into crevices.

Cover and bake for 45 minutes, or until 3 minutes after the aroma of a fully cooked meal escapes the oven. Serve immediately.

Chicken Marsala

The Marsala and fennel seeds give this recipe the familiar flavor of the classic dish, while the red pepper flakes add a bit of a kick. If you are a fennel fan, double the amount given here. You can grind fennel seeds in a mortar or purchase the spice already ground.

Feel free to use any type of fresh or dried mushrooms. Cut dried mushrooms into thin pieces to be certain they will hydrate enough. To presoften particularly thick dried mushrooms, soak them in boiling water for 15 minutes before draining, chopping, and adding to the pot. SERVES 2

Olive oil spray
1 shallot, thinly sliced
4 to 6 garlic cloves, chopped
1 cup whole wheat couscous
$^1/_2$ cup broth (chicken or vegetable)
$^1/_2$ cup Marsala
$^1/_2$ teaspoon red pepper flakes
$^1/_4$ teaspoon ground fennel seeds

$^1/_2$ to $^3/_4$ pound chicken breasts or thighs
1 cup dried porcini mushrooms
1 cup baby carrots, cut into thirds
$^1/_2$ medium zucchini, cut into $^1/_4$-inch slices (about 2 cups)
2 fresh rosemary sprigs

CALORIES 626 • PROTEIN 41G • CARBOHYDRATES 89G • FAT 4G • CHOLESTEROL 77MG • SODIUM 461MG • FIBER 8G

Preheat the oven to 450°F.

Spray the inside and lid of a cast-iron Dutch oven with olive oil.

Sprinkle the shallot and half the garlic in the pot. Add the couscous.

In a small bowl, mix the broth, Marsala, red pepper flakes, and fennel. Pour half the liquid over the couscous. Stir to coat all the grains and make an even layer.

Set the chicken on top of the couscous in a single layer. Pour the rest of the liquid over the chicken and top with the remaining garlic.

Scatter on the mushrooms and carrots.

Stack the zucchini rounds and cut into six wedges (like a pizza). Scatter the wedges on top, filling the pot. Tuck the rosemary sprigs into crevices.

Cover and bake for 45 minutes, or until 3 minutes after the aroma of a fully cooked meal escapes the oven. Serve immediately.

Chicken Piccata

You can use boneless and skinless chicken if you prefer. You can even use frozen boneless chicken pieces without thawing them first. And, of course, use any kind of squash you like, or substitute another vegetable.

If you don't have any broth on hand, you can use water, but you will sacrifice some of the distinctive piccata flavor. Stock your pantry with bouillon cubes or a few cans or boxes of broth. If you have some left over, freeze it in a zip-top freezer bag for another Glorious One-Pot Meal. You can drop the broth in as a frozen slab and it won't change the cooking time. SERVES 2

Olive oil spray

1 cup Arborio rice

1 cup broth (chicken or vegetable)

$^1/_2$ to $^3/_4$ pound chicken breasts or thighs

Sea salt and freshly ground black pepper

1 shallot, or 2 garlic cloves, minced

2 teaspoons chopped fresh parsley

3 tablespoons drained capers

1 lemon

$^1/_2$ red bell pepper, cored, seeded, and sliced into strips

$^1/_2$ head broccoli, cut into florets (about 2 cups)

Preheat the oven to 450°F.

Spray the inside and lid of a cast-iron Dutch oven with olive oil.

Rinse the rice in a strainer under cold water until the water runs clear. Tip the rice into the pot, add the broth and 2 tablespoons water, and stir to make an even layer.

Put the chicken in the pot and lightly season with salt and pepper. Sprinkle with the shallot, parsley, and capers.

Cut the lemon in half and slice one half into rounds, reserving the other half. Top the chicken with a layer of lemon rounds.

Add the bell pepper and broccoli and lightly season with salt and pepper. Squeeze the juice from the other half of the lemon over all, taking care to remove the seeds.

Cover and bake for 45 minutes, or until 3 minutes after the aroma of a fully cooked meal escapes the oven. Serve immediately.

Chicken Satay

My husband declares this dish "insanely good," and he's right. While satay is traditionally broiled or grilled, this Glorious One-Pot Meal version retains all the flavor and skips the hassle of threading skewers, basting, and hovering over a grill.

I sometimes use bouillon cubes to make stock just because they store well and allow you to make any amount you need. Look for low-sodium bouillon cubes in the health food store. Of course, you can use prepared vegetable or chicken broth instead.

Make this recipe hot and spicy by adding a teaspoon of Asian chili sauce or minced hot pepper. Or make it vegetarian by substituting tofu for the chicken. (Be sure to weight the tofu and then blot it with paper towels to remove excess liquid.) SERVES 2

Canola oil spray or sesame oil

1 scallion, white and green parts, sliced into thin rings

2 tablespoons peanut butter

2 tablespoons soy sauce

1 tablespoon light brown sugar

1 tablespoon grated fresh ginger, or $^1/_4$ teaspoon ground

1 or 2 garlic cloves, chopped

1 cup broth (chicken or vegetable)

1 cup rice

$^1/_2$ to $^3/_4$ pound chicken thighs or breasts

$^1/_4$ head red cabbage, shredded (about 2 cups)

About 2 cups fresh or frozen snow pea pods

1 large shiitake mushroom, thinly sliced

CALORIES 400 • PROTEIN 44G • CARBOHYDRATES 46G • FAT 13G • CHOLESTEROL 80MG • SODIUM 1439MG • FIBER 4G

Preheat the oven to 450°F.

Coat the inside and lid of a cast-iron Dutch oven with canola or sesame oil.

In a small bowl, whisk the scallion, peanut butter, soy sauce, brown sugar, ginger, garlic, and 2 tablespoons of the broth. Whisk until the sugar is dissolved and peanut butter is emulsified.

Rinse the rice in a strainer under cold water until the water runs clear. Tip the rice into the pot. Add the remaining broth and $^1/_4$ cup water and stir to make an even layer.

Add the chicken and drizzle with one-third of the peanut butter sauce.

Arrange the cabbage on top and pour half of the remaining sauce over it.

Add the snow peas and mushroom in another layer and pour the rest of the sauce over all.

Cover and bake for 45 minutes, or until 3 minutes after the aroma of a fully cooked meal escapes the oven. Serve immediately. If the rice is still crunchy, fluff with a fork and re-place the lid. Let sit for another 3 to 5 minutes before serving.

Citrus-Ginger Chicken with Root Vegetables

This tangy dish has an unexpectedly sweet, zesty flavor that is a guaranteed crowd-pleaser. I love serving this to company and seeing their surprise when they discover that they've been enjoying turnips and parsnips—vegetables with undeserved bad reputations.

Personally, I prefer to leave the skins of the potatoes, parsnips, and turnips on and simply scrub them well and remove any eyes or bad spots. I try to use organic produce whenever possible, particularly when using whole fruit. Peeling is always optional in an infused one-pot meal, as vegetable skins add many vital nutrients. On the other hand, I prefer to eat chicken without the skin. SERVES 2

Olive or canola oil spray

1 small orange, preferably organic

1 small lemon, preferably organic

2 tablespoons grated fresh ginger, or 1 teaspoon ground

2 tablespoons honey

$^1/_2$ to $^3/_4$ pound chicken thighs or breasts

$^1/_2$ sweet potato, cut into $^1/_2$-inch chunks

$^1/_2$ parsnip, cut into $^1/_4$-inch slices

$^1/_2$ turnip, cut into $^1/_4$-inch slices

6 to 12 asparagus stalks, trimmed and cut into thirds, or $^1/_2$ head broccoli, cut into florets (about 2 cups)

CALORIES 320 • PROTEIN 31G • CARBOHYDRATES 51G • FAT 4G • CHOLESTEROL 81MG • SODIUM 96MG • FIBER 10G

Preheat the oven to 450°F

Spray the inside and lid of a cast-iron Dutch oven with olive or canola oil.

Grate the zest from half of the orange and lemon into a small mixing bowl. Leave the end of the lemon intact. Add the ginger and honey to the bowl.

Slice the orange and lemon in half and squeeze the juice from each scraped half into the bowl. Stir until the honey dissolves.

Slice the remaining halves into thin rounds and arrange them in a single layer in alternating order (orange, lemon, orange, lemon, etc.) to cover the bottom of the pot. Use any remaining slices as a garnish when serving or save for another purpose.

Arrange the chicken on top of the citrus rounds and pour half of the juice mixture over the chicken.

Add the sweet potato, then the parsnip and turnip. Cover with the remainder of the juice mixture, making sure to include the bits of zest and ginger. Top with a final layer of the asparagus.

Cover and bake for 45 minutes, or until 3 minutes after the aroma of a fully cooked meal escapes the oven. Serve immediately.

Frozen Dinner in a Flash

An exceptionally speedy method of producing a healthy and nutritious meal from frozen ingredients, this baseline recipe can be used with a variety of frozen foods. Be sure to keep all ingredients frozen until ready to add to the pot. Try it with frozen fish fillets instead of chicken breasts and Cajun seasoning or salsa instead of teriyaki sauce. In fact, almost any sauce you would use when grilling, such as a barbecue-type sauce or oil-and-vinegar-based salad dressing or marinade, also works well as a flavoring in a Glorious One-Pot Meal.

I keep bags of frozen vegetables in my freezer for convenient Glorious One-Pot Meals. I often mix and match frozen corn, peas and carrots, broccoli, and green beans. Frozen hash browns become similar to chunky mashed potatoes when cooked this way. To make your potatoes smoother and creamier, add $1/4$ cup of liquid, such as water, wine, broth, or even milk. SERVES 2

Canola oil spray

10 to 12 ounces frozen hash browns (not the patties)

Sea salt and freshly ground black pepper

$1/2$ to $3/4$ pound boneless chicken breasts or thighs, frozen separately

$1/4$ cup teriyaki sauce, or more to taste

One 10-ounce bag frozen mixed vegetables

Preheat the oven to 450°F.

Spray the inside and lid of a cast-iron Dutch oven with canola oil.

Shake the hash browns into the pot and season lightly with salt and pepper.

Arrange the chicken on top of the hash browns. Pour the teriyaki sauce over the chicken.

Add enough frozen mixed vegetables to fill the pot. Drizzle with more teriyaki sauce, if desired.

Cover and bake for 45 minutes, or until 3 minutes after the aroma of a fully cooked meal escapes the oven. Serve immediately.

CALORIES 280 • PROTEIN 32G • CARBOHYDRATES 32G • FAT 3G • CHOLESTEROL 75MG • SODIUM 194MG • FIBER 6G

Greek Chicken

This meal sings with the Mediterranean flavors of garlic and olives. Substitute 4 ounces of ripe pitted California olives for the kalamatas, a 14-ounce can of diced tomatoes for fresh tomatoes, and 1¹/2 cups of frozen broccoli florets for the zucchini to change this meal from a taste of summer to an easy midwinter solution without losing the essence of the dish. SERVES 2

Olive oil spray
¹/2 cup couscous
¹/2 cup plus 1 tablespoon broth (chicken or vegetable) or water
¹/2 to ³/4 pound chicken breasts or thighs
Sea salt and freshly ground black pepper
4 to 6 garlic cloves, chopped

1 tablespoon drained capers
2 tablespoons chopped fresh parsley
1 cup pitted kalamata olives, halved
1 medium zucchini, cut into ¹/2-inch slices
3 tomatoes, diced

Preheat the oven to 450°F.

Spray the inside and lid of a cast-iron Dutch oven with olive oil.

Pour the couscous into the pot. Add the liquid and stir to coat all the grains and make an even layer.

Place the chicken on top of the couscous and season lightly with salt and pepper.

Sprinkle with the garlic, capers, and half the parsley. Add the olives, zucchini, and tomatoes.

Sprinkle with the rest of the parsley and lightly season again with salt and pepper.

Cover and bake for 45 minutes, or until 3 minutes after the aroma of a fully cooked meal escapes the oven. Serve immediately.

CALORIES 565 • PROTEIN 34G • CARBOHYDRATES 54G • FAT 24G • CHOLESTEROL 75MG • SODIUM 138MG • FIBER 4G

Red Curry Chicken

Convert this recipe to vegetarian by replacing the chicken with cubes of extra-firm tofu or a 15-ounce can of drained lentils or other beans. Try substituting sweet potatoes for the rice and include eggplant cubes for a truly Indian flair.

   Notice this recipe does not use water to hydrate the rice because the coconut milk in the curry sauce is enough liquid. I find very little difference between regular and light coconut milk in Glorious One-Pot Meals, so use whichever you prefer. You can find red curry paste in the Asian section of your supermarket along with fish sauce and coconut milk. SERVES 2

Canola oil spray

1 cup basmati rice

$^1/_2$ to $^3/_4$ pound chicken breasts or thighs

One 14-ounce can coconut milk, light or regular

2 to 4 tablespoons red curry paste

$1^1/_2$ teaspoons fish sauce

1 teaspoon light brown sugar

Zest of 1 lime, or $^1/_4$ teaspoon lime juice

5 to 10 fresh basil leaves, stems removed, or 1 teaspoon dried

2 carrots, sliced into coins

One 15-ounce can chickpeas, drained and rinsed

2 large handfuls fresh spinach, or one 10-ounce package frozen

CALORIES 1,013 • PROTEIN 43G • CARBOHYDRATES 108G • FAT 45G • CHOLESTEROL 76MG • SODIUM 940MG • FIBER 13G

Preheat the oven to 450°F.

Spray the inside and lid of a cast-iron Dutch oven with canola oil.

Rinse the rice in a strainer under cold water until the water runs clear. Spread the rice in the pot in an even layer. Place the chicken on the rice.

In a medium bowl, whisk the coconut milk, red curry paste, fish sauce, brown sugar, lime zest, and basil. Pour half the mixture over the chicken.

Scatter the carrots and then the chickpeas in the pot. Top with the spinach and pour the rest of the coconut mixture over all.

Cover and bake for 45 minutes, or until 3 minutes after the aroma of a fully cooked meal escapes the oven. Serve immediately. If the rice is still a bit crunchy, quickly fluff with a fork and replace the lid. Let sit for another 3 to 5 minutes before serving.

Moroccan Chicken

Moroccan food has a distinct earthy flavor from the combination of cumin and turmeric. Cinnamon also is a characteristic element here, and raisins add a touch of sweetness.

This recipe also works well using lamb or turkey. SERVES 2

Canola or olive oil spray
1 medium yellow onion, chopped
^{2}/3 cup couscous
1 teaspoon ground cinnamon
^{1}/4 teaspoon ground cumin
^{1}/4 teaspoon ground turmeric
^{1}/2 to ^{3}/4 pound chicken breasts or thighs

^{1}/4 cup raisins
One 8-ounce can tomato sauce
^{1}/2 pound mushrooms, halved or quartered
1 carrot, sliced
2 cups sugar snap peas, halved

Preheat the oven to 450°F.

Spray the inside and lid of a cast-iron Dutch oven with canola or olive oil.

Scatter the onion in the pot.

Put the couscous in a 2-cup measure and add the cinnamon, cumin, and turmeric. Fill with water to the 1^1/2-cup line. Mix well and pour over the onion. Use the back of a spoon to spread the couscous evenly.

Place the chicken on top of the couscous. Sprinkle with raisins. Pour half of the tomato sauce over the top.

Layer in the mushrooms, carrot, and snap peas. Then drizzle the remaining tomato sauce over all.

Cover and bake for 45 minutes, or until 3 minutes after the aroma of a fully cooked meal escapes the oven. Serve immediately.

CALORIES 534 • PROTEIN 41G • CARBOHYDRATES 85G • FAT 5G • CHOLESTEROL 75MG • SODIUM 635MG • FIBER 12G

Pomegranate Chicken

Pomegranate molasses is found in Middle Eastern groceries or dedicated spice shops. You can make your own by boiling down pomegranate juice until it is thick and syrupy.

Look for no-sugar-added peanut butter for a healthier alternative and explore the organic brands when possible. My first choice for nut butters is to stop at the "grind-your-own" peanut or almond butter stations at the health food stores. Try low-sodium soy sauce as well. For a spicy kick, add $^1/_2$ teaspoon of red pepper flakes. SERVES 2

2 teaspoons sesame oil
1 medium sweet potato, cubed
3 or 4 chicken thighs ($^1/_2$ to $^3/_4$ pound)
Sea salt and freshly ground white pepper
2 tablespoons pomegranate molasses
2 tablespoons peanut butter

1 tablespoon soy sauce
$^1/_2$ head broccoli, cut into florets (about 2 cups)
One 15-ounce can diced tomatoes (not drained)

Preheat the oven to 450°F.

Wipe the inside and lid of a cast-iron Dutch oven with sesame oil.

Scatter the sweet potato in the pot. Top with the chicken and lightly season with salt and pepper.

In a small bowl, whisk the pomegranate molasses, peanut butter, and soy sauce. Pour over the chicken.

Add the broccoli in an even layer.

Pour the can of tomatoes and their juice evenly over all.

Cover and bake for 45 minutes, or until 3 minutes after the aroma of a fully cooked meal escapes the oven. Serve immediately.

CALORIES 490 • PROTEIN 36G • CARBOHYDRATES 30G • FAT 16G • CHOLESTEROL 75MG • SODIUM 1125MG • FIBER 7G

One-Pot Thanksgiving

Not everyone wants to cook for an army on the holidays, but there is something about having a traditional holiday meal that evokes a feeling of celebration. This is a great solution to getting the dinner with all the trimmings, yet without spending hours and hours in the kitchen or facing a week of leftovers. Make this any time of year you feel like re-creating these favorite holiday tastes.

The turkey, cranberries, and green beans can all be used fresh or frozen (without thawing) with no change in cooking time. Dried cranberries work, too. In a pinch, substitute pulpy orange juice for the orange marmalade. You'll just end up with more sauce at the bottom of the pot. SERVES 2

Canola oil spray
$^1/_2$ to $^3/_4$ pound turkey tenderloin or boneless breast fillets
Sea salt
$^1/_3$ cup fresh or frozen cranberries
$^1/_3$ cup orange marmalade
1 teaspoon fresh lemon juice
Dash of freshly ground white or black pepper
$^1/_3$ cup walnuts

$^1/_4$ cup chicken broth
8 to 10 fresh or frozen pearl onions (about 2 cups)
1 medium sweet potato or yam, cut into $^1/_4$-inch slices
2 to 4 mushrooms, thickly sliced
2 cups fresh or frozen cut green beans
1 sprig fresh sage, or $^1/_2$ teaspoon dried

CALORIES 494 • PROTEIN 40G • CARBOHYDRATES 52G • FAT 15G • CHOLESTEROL 79MG • SODIUM 275MG • FIBER 7G

Preheat the oven to 450°F.

Spray the inside and lid of a cast-iron Dutch oven with canola oil.

Set the turkey in the pot (if using fillets, try not to overlap the pieces), and lightly season with salt.

In a food processor or blender, pulse the cranberries until they are in small chunks. Add the marmalade, lemon juice, and pepper and pulse two or three times to mix well. Add the walnuts and the broth and continue to pulse until the walnuts are roughly chopped.

Pour about half the cranberry mixture over the turkey. Add the onions, then the sweet potato in a layer and season lightly with salt.

Cover with the rest of the cranberry mixture. Top with the mushrooms and green beans, and tuck the sage sprig into a crevice.

Cover and bake for 38 minutes, or until 3 minutes after the aroma of a Thanksgiving meal escapes the oven. Spoon the sauce from the bottom of the pot over each serving and serve immediately.

Springtime Paella

Paella is a traditional Spanish dish of saffron-infused rice cooked with a variety of meats and vegetables. It varies from season to season and from region to region in Spain. A good paella often contains some crunchy, toasted rice on the bottom of the pot as a counterpoint to the smooth grains.

Typical paellas include a mix of proteins such as chorizo sausage, shrimp, and mussels along with chicken. Feel free to mix and match, using a total of $^1/_2$ to $^3/_4$ pound. This version takes advantage of the springtime arrival of fresh peas and morel mushrooms.

To add a bright note to this recipe, include the grated zest of half a lemon sprinkled on the mushroom layer. Consider substituting white wine for some or all of the liquid. SERVES 2

Olive oil spray

3 garlic cloves, chopped

$^1/_2$ medium onion, sliced thinly

1 cup Arborio or paella rice

1 small pinch saffron threads

$^1/_4$ teaspoon paprika, preferably Spanish smoked pimentón

$^1/_4$ teaspoon red pepper flakes

1 cup plus 1 tablespoon broth (chicken or vegetable) or water, or a mix

$^1/_2$ to $^3/_4$ pound chicken breasts or thighs

Sea salt

$^1/_2$ red bell pepper, cored, seeded, and sliced

2 cups fresh or frozen green peas

3 to 5 morel mushrooms, chopped, optional

8 to 10 cremini mushrooms, sliced

4 to 6 fresh thyme sprigs

CALORIES 608 • PROTEIN 10G • CARBOHYDRATES 97G • FAT 4G • CHOLESTEROL 88MG • SODIUM 173MG • FIBER 4G

Preheat the oven to 450°F.

Spray the inside and lid of a cast-iron Dutch oven with olive oil.

Scatter the garlic and onion in the pot.

Rinse the rice in a strainer until the water runs clear, then add the rice to the pot. Use the back of a spoon to smooth the rice in an even layer.

Add the saffron, paprika, and red pepper flakes to the broth and stir before pouring into the pot.

Add the chicken and season lightly with salt. Cover with a layer of bell pepper, followed by the peas and mushrooms. Set the thyme sprigs on top.

Cover and bake for about 45 minutes, or until 3 minutes after the aroma of a fully cooked meal escapes the oven. Fluff the rice and serve immediately.

Piri-Piri Chicken

This is a perfect dish for a seductively healthy and romantic dinner! What better way to say I love you than sensual pomegranates and healthy brown rice in a sweet but spicy dish? By the way, I consider this a mildly hot meal, while my husband calls it medium-hot. Pomegranate-glazed chicken together with tender pomegranate seeds make an irresistible combination. See page 139 for advice on making your own pomegranate molasses.

A pomegranate is easy to seed if you slice it into quarters and then bend it backward so that the seeds are exposed and easy to grab off the rind. SERVES 2

Olive oil spray

1 cup precooked parboiled brown rice (often sold as "Boil-in-Bag" rice servings)

1 cup broth (chicken or vegetable) or water

$^1/_2$ to $^3/_4$ pound chicken breasts or thighs

Sea salt

$^1/_2$ cup ketchup

2 tablespoons honey

2 tablespoons pomegranate molasses

1 tablespoon fresh lemon juice

2 garlic cloves, chopped

$^1/_4$ teaspoon cayenne

10 to 15 Brussels sprouts (6 to 8 ounces), trimmed with an X in the stem end

$1^1/_2$ cups halved baby carrots

1 cup sliced oyster mushrooms

1 pomegranate, seeded

Preheat the oven to 450°F.

Spray the inside and lid of a cast-iron Dutch oven with olive oil.

Pour the rice into the pot and add the liquid. Stir to coat the grains and smooth the rice into an even layer. Put the chicken pieces on top of the rice. Lightly season with salt.

In a small bowl, mix the ketchup, honey, molasses, lemon juice, garlic, and cayenne. Drizzle half the mixture over the chicken.

Add a layer of Brussels sprouts and carrots. Pour the rest of the ketchup mixture over all. Top with the mushrooms and pomegranate seeds.

Cover and bake for about 45 minutes, or until 3 minutes after the aroma of a fully cooked meal escapes the oven. Serve immediately.

Simply Chicken

With its basic mix of flavors, this recipe is great for kids and other picky eaters. This could easily work as a quick, last-minute dinner of frozen ingredients: a bottom layer of frozen hash browns, then boneless chicken pieces frozen individually, and half a bag of frozen peas and carrots. From the pantry, add dried mushrooms presoaked for about ten minutes in boiling water, then drained. No advance planning needed!

For a bit more flavor, drop in a few halved garlic cloves underneath and around the chicken. Consider drizzling about two tablespoons of your favorite Italian vinaigrette over the chicken instead of salt and pepper for a totally different and inviting flavor combination. SERVES 2

Canola oil spray
$^1/_2$ to $^3/_4$ pound chicken breasts or thighs
Sea salt and freshly ground black pepper

6 to 8 new potatoes, quartered
2 carrots, sliced into coins
4 to 6 mushrooms, thickly sliced
2 cups fresh or frozen green peas

Preheat the oven to 450°F.

Spray the inside and lid of a cast-iron Dutch oven with canola oil.

Put the chicken pieces in the pot, trying not to overlap them, and lightly season with salt and pepper.

Add the potatoes and carrots and again lightly season with salt and pepper.

Scatter the mushrooms in the pot, then pour in the peas.

Cover and bake for 40 to 45 minutes, or until 3 minutes after the aroma of a fully cooked meal escapes the oven. Serve immediately.

CALORIES 440 • PROTEIN 41G • CARBOHYDRATES 47G • FAT 4G • CHOLESTEROL 75MG • SODIUM 331MG • FIBER 15G

Pranzo Italiano

The basic flavors of Italian cooking are olive oil, garlic, oregano, and basil. Add either tomatoes for a hearty ragout, or white wine, parsley, and some lemon for a lighter taste. You can use dried basil and oregano instead of fresh, but you'll need only 1 teaspoon of each. SERVES 2

Olive oil spray

$1/2$ medium onion, halved and thinly sliced

$1/2$ to $3/4$ pound chicken breasts or thighs

$1/2$ head broccoli, cut into florets (about 2 cups)

$1/2$ green bell pepper, cored, seeded, and cut into 1-inch squares

$1/2$ red bell pepper, cored, seeded, and cut into 1-inch squares

5 to 10 mushrooms, sliced

One 14-ounce can diced tomatoes, or 5 fresh tomatoes, chopped

4 or 5 garlic cloves, minced

2 tablespoons chopped fresh basil

2 tablespoons chopped fresh oregano

Preheat the oven to 450°F.

Spray the inside and lid of a cast-iron Dutch oven with olive oil.

Scatter the onion in the pot and top with the chicken.

Add the broccoli, bell peppers, mushrooms, and any other vegetables you choose.

Drain the canned tomatoes, then add the garlic, basil, and oregano to the can and mix well. Spoon this mixture into the pot, targeting any visible crevices.

Cover and bake for 45 minutes, or until 3 minutes after the aroma of a fully cooked meal escapes the oven. Serve immediately.

CALORIES 124 • PROTEIN 15G • CARBOHYDRATES 13G • FAT 2G • CHOLESTEROL 19MG • SODIUM 189MG • FIBER 4G

Chicken Marengo

The story goes that when Napoleon invaded Italy he brought along his own French chef. The army camped at the town of Marengo and the chef created this dish with whatever the scouts brought back from the countryside. Napoleon loved it and the rest, as they say, is history.

Using porcini or other wild mushrooms will give this meal more depth of flavor, but almost any vegetable goes well with the basil and green olives. I like to use penne or farfalle (bow tie pasta) with this recipe, though almost any short pasta should work. SERVES 2

Olive oil spray
1 cup penne or farfalle
$1/2$ teaspoon olive oil
$1/2$ to $3/4$ pound chicken breasts or thighs
Sea salt and freshly ground black pepper
5 garlic cloves, quartered
6 ounces wild mushrooms, sliced

$1/2$ cup small green pimiento-stuffed olives
1 cup fresh or frozen pearl onions
2 tablespoons chopped fresh parsley
1 tablespoon chopped fresh basil
5 to 6 leaves rainbow or Swiss chard, stemmed and chopped (see page 30)
One 14-ounce can diced tomatoes

Preheat the oven to 450°F.

Spray the inside and lid of a cast-iron Dutch oven with olive oil.

Pour the pasta, $1/3$ cup water, and the olive oil into the pot, and stir to coat the noodles.

Arrange the chicken on top and season with salt and pepper. Scatter the garlic on top of the chicken along with the mushrooms, olives, onions, parsley, and basil. Add the chard and pour the entire, undrained can of tomatoes evenly over all.

Cover and bake for 45 minutes, or until 3 minutes after the aroma of a fully cooked meal escapes the oven. Serve immediately.

CALORIES 335 • PROTEIN 34G • CARBOHYDRATES 37G • FAT 6G • CHOLESTEROL 75MG • SODIUM 926MG • FIBER 5G

Scarborough Fair Chicken

Inspired by the classic tune, all this dish is missing is the rosemary; it's too strong a flavor for this meal.

Keeping the sprigs of herbs intact streamlines the preparation. The flavors mingle and infuse the food even though the leaves are still on the stems. Be sure to remove the thyme sprigs before serving; the stems are too woody to eat. SERVES 2

Olive oil spray

1 cup white rice

1 cup plus 1 tablespoon broth (chicken or vegetable) or water

$^1/_2$ to $^3/_4$ pound chicken breasts or thighs

Sea salt and freshly ground black pepper

3 to 5 garlic cloves, chopped

3 to 5 shallots, chopped

1 medium zucchini, cut into $^1/_2$-inch slices

1 medium yellow squash, cut into $^1/_2$-inch slices

5 fresh parsley sprigs

3 fresh sage leaves

4 fresh thyme sprigs

Preheat the oven to 450°F.

Spray the inside and lid of a cast-iron Dutch oven with olive oil.

Rinse the rice in a strainer under cold water until the water runs clear. Pour the rice and liquid into the pot. Stir to make an even layer.

Place the chicken on the rice and season lightly with salt and pepper. Sprinkle with the garlic and shallots.

Add the zucchini and squash. Scatter on the parsley and sage and tuck the thyme sprigs in crevices.

Cover and bake for 45 minutes, or until 3 minutes after the aroma of a fully cooked meal escapes the oven. Serve immediately.

CALORIES 459 • PROTEIN 34G • CARBOHYDRATES 76G • FAT 5G • CHOLESTEROL 75MG • SODIUM 54MG • FIBER 4G

Rosemary Chicken

I like to think of this recipe as comfort food without all the pots and pans. In the Western tradition, rosemary has traditionally been a symbol of friendship, love, and remembrance. In Chinese medicine, the evergreen herb is used as a warming remedy. Either way, this meal is guaranteed to bring a sense of warmth and security to all who partake.

To prepare acorn squash, cut off the top and bottom ends and cut in half. Then scoop out the seeds and strings with a spoon. Cut into wedges and peel. Or cook with the peel on, as it will easily come off once cooked. The deep orange of this squash boosts your intake of vitamins A and C.

If using very large potatoes, cut into one-inch cubes to be sure they cook through. The smaller the cubes, the more thoroughly they will cook. SERVES 2

Canola or olive oil spray
$^1/_2$ medium onion, cut into 1-inch slices
$^1/_2$ to $^3/_4$ pound chicken breasts or thighs
Sea salt and freshly ground black pepper
6 to 8 small red potatoes, quartered

$^1/_2$ small acorn squash, cut into 1-inch cubes
5 to 10 mushrooms, thickly sliced
2 cups fresh or frozen cut green beans
4 to 6 small fresh rosemary sprigs, or $^1/_2$ teaspoon dried

CALORIES 339 • PROTEIN 35G • CARBOHYDRATES 59G • FAT 3G • CHOLESTEROL 5MG • SODIUM 53MG • FIBER 8G

Preheat the oven to 450°F.

Spray the inside and lid of a cast-iron Dutch oven with canola or olive oil.

Separate the onion slices and scatter in the pot.

Place the chicken on the onion and season lightly with salt and pepper.

Arrange the potatoes around the chicken. Layer the squash over the chicken and add the mushrooms. Cover with a final even layer of green beans and lightly season with salt and pepper. Tuck the rosemary sprigs into crevices.

Cover and bake for 45 minutes, or until 3 minutes after the aroma of a fully cooked meal escapes the oven. Serve immediately.

Santa Fe Chicken

I became a green chile addict when I lived in New Mexico. Home in Colorado, I buy them by the freshly roasted bushel in the fall and freeze them in one-quart plastic bags so I can always get that green chile fix when I need it.

This is a great meal to make when you don't have any fresh vegetables in the house. Stock up on the canned or frozen ingredients and you'll be able to whip up this Southwestern staple in a jiffy. You can use bone-in or boneless, skin-on or skinless, fresh or frozen chicken pieces; they will still take the same amount of time to cook.

You can control the amount of spiciness by the type and amount of chile peppers or salsa you decide to use. My personal favorites are Hatch green chiles, but any chile works. Or use your favorite salsa. SERVES 2

Canola oil spray

One 15-ounce can black beans, drained and rinsed

1 scallion, white and green parts, thinly sliced

$^1/_2$ to $^3/_4$ pound chicken breasts or thighs

One 4-ounce can green chiles, or 4 to 6 tablespoons prepared salsa

$^1/_2$ green bell pepper, cored, seeded, and cut into 1-inch strips

One 14-ounce bag frozen corn, or one 15-ounce can, drained

One 14-ounce can diced tomatoes, drained

One 6-ounce can sliced black olives

Preheat the oven to 450°F.

Spray the inside and lid of a cast-iron Dutch oven with canola oil.

Spread the beans in an even layer in the pot.

Arrange the scallion on top of the beans, then add the chicken. If you're using green chiles, blanket the chicken with them. If you're using salsa, spoon it over the chicken.

Add the bell pepper, corn, tomatoes, and olives in separate even layers.

Cover and bake for 45 minutes, or until 3 minutes after the aroma of a fully cooked meal escapes the oven. Serve immediately.

Savory Port-Mushroom Chicken

Try this recipe with steak or tempeh or even veal. Spoon any residual broth over the chicken before serving and remember to remove the rosemary sprig. SERVES 2

Olive oil spray

$^1/_4$ medium onion, thinly sliced

1 cup bow tie pasta (farfalle)

$^1/_2$ to $^3/_4$ pound chicken breasts or thighs

Sea salt and freshly ground black pepper

1 large portobello mushroom, halved and thinly sliced

2 tablespoons ruby port

1 teaspoon balsamic vinegar

1 teapoon Worcestershire sauce

$^1/_2$ teaspoon Dijon mustard

2 teaspoons olive oil

2 carrots, sliced into coins

One 3-inch fresh rosemary sprig, or 1 teaspoon dried

2 cups cut green beans or snow pea pods

CALORIES 330 • PROTEIN 33G • CARBOHYDRATES 35G • FAT 6G • CHOLESTEROL 75MG • SODIUM 135MG • FIBER 4G

Preheat the oven to 450°F.

Spray the inside and lid of a cast-iron Dutch oven with olive oil.

Scatter the onion in the pot. Add the pasta and $^1/_3$ cup of water. Stir to coat the noodles and distribute them in an even layer.

Add the chicken to the pot and lightly season with salt and pepper. Arrange the mushrooms in a layer on top of the chicken.

In a measuring cup, mix the port, vinegar, Worcestershire sauce, mustard, olive oil, and 1 tablespoon of water. Stir with a whisk or fork to emulsify the mustard, then drizzle into the pot.

Add the carrots and tuck the rosemary sprig into a crevice. Top with a layer of green beans.

Cover and bake for 45 minutes, or until 3 minutes after the aroma of a fully cooked meal escapes the oven. Serve immediately.

Stuffed Cabbage

My grandmother used to spend all day making her Old World cabbage rolls stuffed with ground beef, onions, rice, and raisins. We all loved them, but I don't have the time or the patience to do it her way. Feel free to substitute chopped mushrooms in place of the ground meat for a vegetarian version. Hope you enjoy my take on this heirloom recipe! SERVES 2

Olive oil spray
$^1/_4$ cup hulled or pearl barley
Sea salt and freshly ground black pepper
6 to 8 intact green cabbage leaves
One 14-ounce can diced tomatoes
Juice of 1 lemon
1 tablespoon light brown sugar, optional

1 large egg
$^1/_2$ medium onion, chopped
1 carrot, grated or minced
$^1/_2$ to $^3/_4$ pound ground turkey or beef
1 tablespoon minced fresh parsley
1 to 3 garlic cloves, minced
$^1/_4$ cup raisins, optional

Preheat the oven to 450°F.

Spray the inside and lid of a cast-iron Dutch oven with olive oil.

Using a strainer, rinse the barley under cold water. Pour the barley into the pot along with $^1/_2$ cup water. Lightly season with salt and pepper.

Arrange a layer of cabbage leaves on top of the barley.

Drain the tomatoes into a small bowl. Stir the lemon juice into the tomato liquid, add the sugar if desired, and lightly season with salt and pepper.

Gently beat the egg in a medium mixing bowl. Add the onion, carrot, turkey, parsley, and garlic; mix well. Fold in the tomatoes and lightly season with salt and pepper.

Drop in half of the ground meat mixture by forkfuls, making an even layer. Pour in half of the tomato juice mixture evenly. Sprinkle with the raisins, if using.

Add a layer of cabbage leaves and the rest of the meat mixture. Cover with any leftover cabbage leaves and pour the rest of the tomato juice mixture over all.

Cover and bake for 45 minutes, or until 3 minutes after the aroma of a fully cooked meal escapes the oven. Serve immediately.

Sweet-Tart Chicken

Pomegranate molasses has a taste that is sweet but with a tartness reminiscent of cranberries that is satisfying for the kid in all of us. Great with boneless, skinless thighs, this chicken dish is glazed with flavor. Don't forget to spoon the sauce at the bottom of the pot over each serving as you won't want to miss a drop! (See page 139 for a discussion of pomegranate molasses.)

Brussels sprouts that touch the side or lid of the pot may get some roasted leaves. If you prefer to avoid this, simply keep them away from the edges of the pot or cover with sauce. SERVES 2

Canola oil spray

$^1/_2$ medium onion, halved and sliced

3 or 4 chicken thighs ($^1/_2$ to $^3/_4$ pound)

Sea salt and freshly ground black pepper

2 tablespoons pomegranate molasses

2 tablespoons whole-grain mustard

2 or 3 unpeeled boiling potatoes, cut into 1-inch cubes

$^1/_3$ acorn squash, peeled or not, seeded, and cut in large chunks

6 ounces Brussels sprouts, trimmed and halved lengthwise

4 to 6 cremini mushrooms, thickly sliced

CALORIES 305 • PROTEIN 31G • CARBOHYDRATES 41G • FAT 4G • CHOLESTEROL 75MG • SODIUM 189MG • FIBER 5G

Preheat the oven to 450°F.

Spray the inside and lid of a cast-iron Dutch oven with canola oil.

Scatter the onion evenly in the pot.

Arrange the chicken in a layer and lightly season with salt.

In a small bowl, whisk the pomegranate molasses and mustard until the mustard is almost emulsified. Pour half the mixture over the chicken.

Arrange the potatoes on top, followed by the squash, and lightly season with salt and pepper. Scatter the Brussels sprouts over the squash, then top with the mushrooms. Pour the rest of the mustard mixture over all.

Cover and bake for about 45 minutes, or until 3 minutes after the aroma of a fully cooked meal escapes the oven. Serve immediately.

Thai Chicken

Sometimes I like to enhance the Thai flavor of this recipe by adding a few sprigs of mint to the pot. If you can find Thai basil, that would add even more authenticity. To make this even spicier, increase the amount of sweet chili sauce by $1/2$ teaspoon. Find sweet chili sauce along with fish sauce in the Asian section of the grocery store or at an Asian market. SERVES 2

Canola oil spray

1 cup white rice

1 cup plus 1 tablespoon broth (chicken or vegetable) or water

$1/2$ to $3/4$ pound chicken breasts or thighs or chicken strips

2 tablespoons hoisin sauce

1 tablespoon chopped fresh cilantro

1 to $1^1/2$ teaspoons Asian fish sauce

$1/2$ teaspoon sweet chili sauce

$1/4$ teaspoon ground coriander

$1/4$ teaspoon sea salt

Freshly ground white pepper

One 6-ounce can bamboo shoots, drained

$1/2$ red bell pepper, cored, seeded, and cut into strips

2 cups fresh or frozen cut green or yellow string beans

1 head baby bok choy, trimmed and roughly chopped

Preheat the oven to 450°F.

Spray the inside and lid of a cast-iron Dutch oven with canola oil.

Rinse the rice in a strainer under cold water until the water runs clear and pour into the pot. Add the liquid, and stir to make an even layer. Add the chicken.

In a small bowl, stir together the hoisin sauce, cilantro, fish sauce, chili sauce, coriander, salt, and pepper. Pour over the chicken.

Scatter the bamboo shoots over the chicken. Add the bell pepper, followed by the beans. Top with the bok choy until the pot is full.

Cover and bake for 45 minutes, or until 3 minutes after the aroma of a fully cooked meal escapes the oven. Serve immediately.

CALORIES 539 • PROTEIN 36G • CARBOHYDRATES 94G • FAT 6G • CHOLESTEROL 75MG • SODIUM 894MG • FIBER 6G

VEGETARIAN

Aegean Eggplant

This recipe reminds me of lightly cooked and dressed salads shared under the endless skies above the Greek isles. I spent one summer during college working in a restaurant on the island of Rhodes and found many opportunities to savor the Greek flavors. To truly get into the spirit, you'd have to serve dinner with candlelight, plenty of retsina, and lots of laughter!

For firmer, more al dente lentils, use $^1/_2$ cup dry lentils and 1 cup of liquid instead of canned.

SERVES 2

Olive oil spray

1 cup white rice

1 cup vegetable broth

One 15-ounce can lentils, drained and rinsed

$^1/_2$ medium onion, chopped

$^1/_2$ medium eggplant (cut lengthwise)

3 garlic cloves, thinly sliced

$^1/_4$ teaspoon paprika

Freshly ground black pepper

2 teaspoons chopped fresh parsley

1 tablespoon drained capers

4 to 6 Swiss chard leaves, stems separated from leaves (see page 30)

2 tablespoons red wine vinegar

$^1/_2$ teaspoon ground nutmeg

CALORIES 415 • PROTEIN 16G • CARBOHYDRATES 89G • FAT 2G • CHOLESTEROL 0 • SODIUM 773MG • FIBER 7G

Preheat the oven to 450°F.

Spray the inside and lid of a cast-iron Dutch oven with olive oil.

Rinse the rice in a strainer under cold water until the water runs clear. Pour the rice and broth into the pot. Stir to coat the grains and make an even layer.

Spread the lentils in the pot in an even layer. Scatter the onion on top of the lentils.

Cut the eggplant horizontally into $^1\!/4$- to $^1\!/2$-inch slices, then cut the slices in half. Arrange the wedges in a layer. Scatter the garlic on top of the eggplant. Sprinkle with the paprika, pepper, and parsley, then scatter in the capers.

Mince the chard stems and scatter them evenly in the pot. Drizzle with the vinegar. Roughly cut the chard leaves and pack them into the pot; sprinkle with nutmeg and more pepper.

Cover and bake for 35 minutes, or until 3 minutes after the aroma of a fully cooked meal escapes the oven. Serve immediately.

Aloo Gobi

This Glorious One-Pot Meal is a take on a traditional Indian dish. Consider changing it up with chicken, sweet potatoes, and broccoli in place of chickpeas, white potato, and cauliflower.

Turmeric has anti-inflammatory properties and may be helpful for people suffering from internal swelling of joints or nerves, as with fibromyalgia, arthritis, and multiple sclerosis. SERVES 2

Canola oil spray
$^1/_8$ teaspoon black mustard seeds
1 cup jasmine rice
$^1/_2$ medium onion, thinly sliced
One 15-ounce can chickpeas, drained and rinsed
$^1/_8$ teaspoon ground turmeric
$^1/_2$ teaspoon ground cumin
$^1/_2$ teaspoon ground coriander

$^3/_4$ teaspoon garam masala
1 teaspoon grated fresh ginger
$^1/_2$ teaspoon sugar
2 tomatoes, chopped
2 handfuls fresh baby spinach leaves, chopped
1 potato, cubed
2 cups cauliflower florets

CALORIES 649 • PROTEIN 19G • CARBOHYDRATES 131G • FAT 6G • CHOLESTEROL 0 • SODIUM 691 MG • FIBER 22G

Preheat the oven to 450°F.

Spray the inside and lid of a cast-iron Dutch oven with canola oil.

Sprinkle the mustard seeds in the bottom of the pot.

Rinse the rice in a strainer under cold water until the water runs clear. Tip the rice into the pot and spread in an even layer. Add 1 cup plus 1 tablespoon water.

Scatter on the onion and evenly spread the chickpeas on top.

In a small bowl, mix the turmeric, cumin, coriander, garam masala, ginger, and sugar. Fold in the tomatoes and spinach and pour half the mixture over the chickpeas.

Create a layer of potato and then a layer of cauliflower. Pour the rest of the tomato mixture over all.

Cover and bake for 45 minutes, or until 3 minutes after the aroma of a fully cooked meal escapes the oven. Serve immediately.

Artichoke and Mushroom Pasta

Feel free to experiment with cheeses besides Parmesan. Try mozzarella, feta, or provolone—each makes a completely different meal.

Fresh wild mushrooms, such as chanterelle or shiitake, add a complex, earthy flavor, but dried mushrooms work well, too, and may be easier to find. I like to keep dried wild mushrooms in my pantry for spur-of-the-moment dishes. Sometimes I place them in a bowl, cover with boiling water, and let sit for fifteen minutes to soften, then drain and use. Other times I simply chop the dried mushrooms and throw them into the pot for a chewier version that adds another texture to the meal. SERVES 2

Olive oil spray

3 to 5 garlic cloves, chopped

$1/2$ medium yellow onion, thinly sliced

2 cups rotini, fusilli, penne, or other short pasta

$1/3$ cup sherry

$1/3$ cup broth (vegetable or chicken) or water

One 14-ounce can artichokes packed in water, drained

1 tablespoon chopped fresh thyme

Sea salt and freshly ground black pepper

2 medium tomatoes, roughly chopped

$1/4$ cup grated Parmesan cheese, optional

3 cups sliced fresh wild mushrooms, or $1^1/2$ cups dried

Preheat the oven to 450°F.

Spray the inside and lid of a cast-iron Dutch oven with olive oil.

Sprinkle the garlic in the pot, then scatter in the onion.

Pour in the pasta, sherry, and liquid. Stir gently to coat the noodles and spread them evenly. Arrange the artichokes in a layer. Sprinkle with thyme and lightly season with salt and pepper.

Add the tomatoes. If desired, shower with Parmesan. Top with the mushrooms.

Cover and bake for about 35 minutes, or until 3 minutes after the aroma of a fully cooked meal escapes the oven. Serve immediately.

Boulder Polenta

Tofu is like a sponge and will absorb whatever flavors you give it if you squeeze it dry first. I often sandwich the block of tofu between several layers of paper towels and then set the Dutch oven on top to press out as much liquid as possible. If you're not into tofu, substitute eight ounces of ricotta cheese.

Using freshly grated nutmeg is always a treat. I keep a few whole nutmegs in a jar and simply run one across a Microplane grater. Save the rest of the nut in a jar so it will be fresh and aromatic the next time you want it. A whole nutmeg can last a year or longer.

Try to break a block of frozen spinach into pieces before adding it to the pot, and realize that it will add some liquid as it melts. Let the pot sit for a few minutes with the lid off before serving to allow the polenta to absorb any extra liquid. SERVES 2

Olive oil spray

1/2 cup dry polenta

1 1/2 cups broth (vegetable or chicken) or water

6 to 10 ounces extra-firm or firm tofu, drained and pressed (see headnote)

3 to 4 tablespoons grated Parmesan or pecorino Romano cheese

4 ounces mozzarella cheese, grated or in chunks

4 to 6 garlic cloves, minced

1/2 teaspoon dried basil

1 tablespoon drained capers

8 ounces pitted black olives, sliced

One 10-ounce package frozen spinach, or 2 large handfuls fresh

4 to 8 mushrooms, fresh or dried, coarsely chopped

1/2 teaspoon grated nutmeg

CALORIES 698 • PROTEIN 24G • CARBOHYDRATES 51G • FAT 44G • CHOLESTEROL 57MG • SODIUM 3093MG • FIBER 1G

Preheat the oven to 450°F.

Spray the inside and lid of a cast-iron Dutch oven with olive oil.

Pour the polenta and the liquid into the pot and stir to spread the polenta evenly.

In a medium mixing bowl, crumble the tofu into chunks (it should resemble ricotta cheese) and stir together with the cheeses. Add the garlic, basil, capers, and olives and mix lightly. If using fresh spinach, fold it into the mixture. If the spinach is a frozen block, chop it into large pieces and set them in the pot next so the other ingredients can be piled around the chunks. Then spoon half of the tofu mixture into the pot.

Scatter the mushrooms and top with the rest of the tofu mixture. Sprinkle with nutmeg.

Cover and bake for 45 minutes, or until 3 minutes after the aroma of a fully cooked meal escapes the oven. Serve immediately.

Curried Veggies

A vegetarian dish brimming with Indian flavors, this recipe reminds me of a meal I ate in a London restaurant after enjoying a rip-roaring rock musical in Soho. I hope you have as much fun eating this one as I did that night!

For an even healthier meal, use parboiled and precooked brown rice (labeled "instant") with the same amount of liquid. SERVES 2

Canola oil spray

2 garlic cloves, chopped

1/4 medium onion, halved and sliced

1 fresh jalapeño chile, stemmed, seeded, and chopped

1 cup basmati rice

1 cup plus 1 tablespoon vegetable broth

1/2 teaspoon garam masala

1/2 teaspoon ground turmeric

1/2 teaspoon ground cumin

2 carrots, sliced into coins

1 parsnip, sliced into coins

2 cups cauliflower florets

1 medium zucchini, halved lengthwise and cut into 1/2-inch slices

2 cups fresh or frozen green peas

CALORIES 567 • PROTEIN 21G • CARBOHYDRATES 105G • FAT 1G • CHOLESTEROL 0 • SODIUM 314MG • FIBER 20G

Preheat the oven to 450°F.

Spray the inside and lid of a cast-iron Dutch oven with canola oil.

Scatter the garlic, onion, and chile in the pot.

Rinse the rice in a strainer under cold water until the water runs clear, then add to the pot.

In a measuring cup, stir together the broth, garam masala, turmeric, and cumin. Pour two-thirds of the broth over the rice. Stir the rice to coat the grains and spread them evenly.

Add the carrots, parsnip, cauliflower, zucchini, and peas in layers in this order. Pour the rest of the broth-spice mixture over all.

Cover and bake for 45 minutes, or until 3 minutes after the aroma of a fully cooked meal escapes the oven. Serve immediately.

Eggplant Parmesan

While my mother wouldn't be caught dead serving jarred marinara sauce, I've found quality organic brands speed up prep time and taste as good as homemade. Sometimes I'll doctor the sauce with fresh tomatoes, zucchini, or green peppers from the garden. Or I'll add roasted green chiles (available frozen, canned, or fresh in the fall) or red pepper flakes for a flavor boost.

If using a nondairy cheese, be aware that brands containing casein retain more of the creaminess associated with real cheese than those without. While the presence of casein shouldn't affect most lactose-intolerant people, it is an animal product and could cause those allergic to dairy to have a reaction.

Instead of using prepared marinara sauce, you could stir the herbs directly into a can of crushed tomatoes and pour this mixture over the layers of eggplant. SERVES 2

Olive oil spray

1 cup elbow macaroni

3 to 6 garlic cloves, minced

1/4 teaspoon dried oregano

1/4 teaspoon dried basil, or 1 tablespoon chopped fresh

Sea salt and freshly ground black pepper

8 to 12 ounces prepared marinara sauce

1 small eggplant, peeled or not, cut into 1-inch cubes (about 2 cups)

8 to 10 ounces mozzarella and/or provolone cheeses, shredded or sliced

4 or 5 cremini mushrooms, sliced

Spinach, artichoke hearts, black olives, or other veggies, optional

Grated Parmesan cheese, optional

Bread crumbs, optional

Preheat the oven to 450°F.

Spray the inside and lid of a cast-iron Dutch oven with olive oil.

Place the pasta in the pot and add $^1/_3$ cup water. Stir to coat the noodles and spread them in an even layer.

Mix the garlic, oregano, basil, and salt and pepper into the jar of marinara sauce. Layer about half the eggplant in the pot and cover it in marinara sauce.

Next distribute a light blanket of cheese (about half) over the sauce. Add a layer of the mushrooms and other veggies such as artichoke hearts and olives, if desired.

Repeat, beginning with the eggplant layer, until the pot is full. Sprinkle with Parmesan and/or bread crumbs, if desired.

Cover and bake for about 40 minutes, or until 3 minutes after the aroma of a fully cooked meal escapes the oven. Serve immediately.

Eggplant with Garlic Sauce and Sticky Rice

Eggplant with garlic sauce is one of my favorite dishes at Chinese restaurants. This version tastes slightly different because it is not wok-fried; it is much less oily than the traditional version but has a similar sweet/spicy/salty sauce. I like to use sushi rice in this recipe, but any kind of white rice or even parboiled precooked brown rice will work. Use this recipe to make almost anything with garlic sauce—broccoli, tofu, chicken, or whatever you like.

Edamame are soybeans. The Japanese traditionally like to munch on these, boiled and salted, as a healthy source of protein.

If you aren't familiar with jicama, try it—it is a light, crunchy, slightly starchy root vegetable. It peels easily with a vegetable peeler and is wonderful raw in salads or as a crudité. If not using jicama, substitute carrots or celery in thin strips or a four-ounce can of sliced bamboo shoots, drained. SERVES 2

2 teaspoons sesame oil

1 cup sushi rice

1 cup plus 2 tablespoons vegetable broth

1 small eggplant, peeled or not, cut into 1-inch cubes (about 2 cups)

2 scallions, white and green parts, cut diagonally into 1-inch lengths

Sea salt

4 to 6 garlic cloves, chopped

$1/4$ cup soy sauce

2 tablespoons sugar

1 tablespoon rice vinegar

1 tablespoon sake or dry sherry

$1/2$ teaspoon chili oil

1 tablespoon cornstarch

1 teaspoon red pepper flakes, optional

$1/4$ jicama, peeled and julienned (see page 74 for a description of how to cut julienne-style sticks)

$1/2$ red bell pepper, cored, seeded, and cut in bite-size pieces

1 cup fresh or frozen edamame, shelled

CALORIES 668 • PROTEIN 26G • CARBOHYDRATES 114G • FAT 13G • CHOLESTEROL 0 • SODIUM 2458MG • FIBER 11G

Preheat the oven to 450°F.

Wipe the inside and lid of a cast-iron Dutch oven with sesame oil.

Rinse the rice in a strainer under cold water until the water runs clear. Tip the rice into the pot, add 1 cup of the broth, and stir to make an even layer.

Add the eggplant and sprinkle with scallions. Salt liberally ($^1/_8$ to $^1/_4$ teaspoon), keeping in mind that the soy sauce will also add quite a bit of salt.

In a small bowl, mix the garlic, soy sauce, sugar, vinegar, sake, chili oil, cornstarch, the remaining 2 tablespoons of broth, and the red pepper flakes. Mix well to dissolve the cornstarch and sugar. Pour half the mixture over the eggplant, distributing evenly.

Add the jicama and bell pepper to the pot. Scatter on the edamame. Pour the rest of the soy mixture over all.

Cover and bake for 45 minutes, or until 3 minutes after the aroma of a fully cooked meal escapes the oven. If there are still crunchy spots in your rice, leave the pot covered for 3 to 5 minutes after removing it from the oven. If there is too much extra liquid, remove the lid and let sit for 3 to 5 minutes before serving.

Glorious Macaroni and Cheese

This is a mac-and-cheese you can actually feel good about serving. Substitute any vegetables you prefer to boost the nutrition of this meal far beyond any boxed version bought at the store.

Traditionally, American-style macaroni and cheese is made primarily with Cheddar cheese, but personally I'm a fan of using mozzarella and Monterey Jack. Of course, you can mix and match any combination of cheeses in this meal. Nondairy cheeses perform about as well as real cheeses in Glorious One-Pot Meals, although I usually look for those listing casein as an ingredient for that cheesy gooeyness that's more like the real stuff. Casein might be a problem for vegans and those with mild dairy allergies, so keep this in mind.

You can use much less cheese than I recommend and the dish will still turn out pretty cheesy. If you find it is too rich, try using harder, lower-fat cheeses such as Swiss, provolone, or Parmesan. Enjoy experimenting with your favorite cheeses.

Some noodles and cheese may form a crusty layer along the bottom and lower sides of the pot. While my husband enjoys crunching these tasty strips, stirring well to coat the noodles with water when building the pot and paying careful attention to when the aroma first escapes the oven will help you avoid this. SERVES 2

Olive oil spray

2 cups macaroni

1/2 teaspoon olive oil

8 to 12 ounces cheese, such as Cheddar, mozzarella, or Monterey Jack, sliced or grated

3 to 5 garlic cloves, chopped

1 tablespoon chopped fresh oregano, or 1/2 teaspoon dried

Sea salt and freshly ground black pepper

1/2 yellow bell pepper, cored, seeded, and cut into thin strips

1/2 head broccoli, cut into florets (about 2 cups)

2 handfuls fresh spinach, shredded (about 2 loosely packed cups)

2 or 3 plum tomatoes, chopped, or one 14-ounce can, drained, liquid reserved, optional

CALORIES 535 • PROTEIN 24G • CARBOHYDRATES 60G • FAT 23G • CHOLESTEROL 60MG • SODIUM 438MG • FIBER 6G

Preheat the oven to 450°F.

Spray the inside and lid of a cast-iron Dutch oven with olive oil, taking care to fully coat all interior surfaces.

Pour the pasta into the pot.

Combine $2/3$ cup water and the olive oil in a measuring cup. (If using canned tomatoes, drain and use the liquid to replace the water.) Stir and pour over the pasta. Mix gently to coat all the noodles and spread them evenly in the pot.

Layer about half the cheese over the pasta. Sprinkle with half the garlic and half the oregano and lightly season with salt and pepper.

Add the bell pepper and broccoli in even layers and cover with the remaining cheese. Sprinkle with the remaining garlic and oregano and season lightly with salt and pepper.

Top with the spinach and, if you choose, tomatoes.

Cover and bake for 30 minutes, or until 3 minutes after the aroma of a fully cooked meal escapes the oven. Serve immediately.

Farmhouse Pasta

Want to add meat to this meal? Consider strips of salami or prosciutto. SERVES 2

Olive oil spray
1/4 cup pine nuts
2 cups rigatoni or other tubular pasta
1/2 teaspoon olive oil
1/4 medium red onion, sliced
4 ounces soft goat cheese
1/4 cup oil-packed sun-dried tomatoes, chopped

1/4 teaspoon red pepper flakes
1 tablespoon chopped fresh basil
3 tablespoons balsamic vinegar
5 mushrooms, sliced
5 to 7 large kale leaves, stemmed and roughly chopped (about 2 cups; see page 30 for advice on removing stems)

Preheat the oven to 450°F.

Spray the inside and lid of a cast-iron Dutch oven with olive oil.

While the oven is preheating, place the pine nuts on a cookie sheet in the oven to lightly toast. Keep an eye on them, as they will take only a couple of minutes to turn golden. Remove from the oven and let cool.

Pour the pasta into the pot, add 2/3 cup water, and stir to make an even layer.

Scatter on the onion and distribute the goat cheese in chunks.

Distribute the sun-dried tomatoes on top of the cheese and sprinkle with the red pepper flakes, basil, and vinegar.

Add the mushrooms and finish with as much kale as you can fit into the pot. Make sure the lid fits tightly.

Cover and bake for 45 minutes, or until 3 minutes after the aroma of a fully cooked meal escapes the oven. Serve immediately.

CALORIES 476 • PROTEIN 18G • CARBOHYDRATES 61G • FAT 19G • CHOLESTEROL 10MG • SODIUM 299MG • FIBER 5G

Greek Eggplant with Bread Stuffing

This is a complete and hearty vegetarian meal. To make this meal vegan, just omit the feta cheese or use a soy or rice cheese substitute. Try this dish with mozzarella cheese for a different flavor combination. SERVES 2

Olive oil spray

1/2 medium onion, finely chopped

1/2 red bell pepper, cored, seeded, and finely chopped

One 14-ounce can diced tomatoes, drained

1 tablespoon chopped fresh oregano, or 1 teaspoon dried

4 to 6 garlic cloves, minced

2 tablespoons chopped fresh parsley

1/2 cup bread crumbs

Freshly ground black pepper

1 medium eggplant, peeled or not, cut into 1-inch cubes (about 2 cups)

3 ounces feta cheese, crumbled

One 15-ounce can chickpeas, drained and rinsed

Preheat the oven to 450°F.

Spray the inside and lid of a cast-iron Dutch oven with olive oil.

In a medium bowl, mix the onion, bell pepper, tomatoes, oregano, garlic, parsley, and bread crumbs. Season with pepper to taste.

Arrange half of the eggplant in a layer in the pot.

Blanket with half of the feta, spoon in half the bread crumb mixture, and top with half of the chickpeas.

Repeat the layers with the rest of the ingredients.

Cover and bake for 45 minutes, or until 3 minutes after the aroma of a fully cooked meal escapes the oven. Serve immediately.

CALORIES 535 • PROTEIN 24G • CARBOHYDRATES 71G • FAT 16G • CHOLESTEROL 30MG • SODIUM 178MG • FIBER 21G

Indian Tofu

You can control the amount of heat in this meal with the types and amounts of chile peppers. I like the spectrum of flavors that results from mixing roasted with fresh chiles.

To roast a chile pepper, you can treat it as you would a marshmallow when camping, using tongs or a long fork to rotate it over a low flame on a gas burner. However, a safer chile-roasting method is to place the chile on a baking sheet and slide it under the broiler for just a few minutes. When charred on all sides, place the chile in a bowl and cover with plastic wrap. The steaming will loosen the skin, making it easy to remove. Peel, stem, and seed roasted peppers before using.

See page 168 for a discussion on preparing tofu. SERVES 2

Olive oil spray

1 cup basmati rice

6 to 8 ounces extra-firm tofu, drained and pressed

1/2 cup dry red wine

1 serrano chile, stemmed, seeded, and chopped

1/2 teaspoon garam masala

1/2 teaspoon ground turmeric

1/4 teaspoon ground cumin

1/8 teaspoon sea salt

1/4 medium onion, chopped

One 15-ounce can lentils, drained and rinsed

1 large Anaheim green chile, roasted, stemmed, seeded, peeled, and chopped (see headnote)

2 cups bite-size cauliflower florets

1/2 medium zucchini, quartered lengthwise and thickly sliced (about 2 cups)

2 or 3 medium tomatoes, diced, or one 14-ounce can, drained and chopped

CALORIES 610 • PROTEIN 25G • CARBOHYDRATES 107G • FAT 4G • CHOLESTEROL 0 • SODIUM 968MG • FIBER 12G

Preheat the oven to 450°F.

Spray the inside and lid of a cast-iron Dutch oven with olive oil.

Rinse the rice in a strainer under cold water until the water runs clear. Pour the rice into the pot. Add 1 cup plus 1 tablespoon water (or vegetable broth) and stir to coat the grains and spread them in an even layer.

Squeeze the tofu as dry as possible and cut into 1-inch cubes. Place in a medium bowl.

In a measuring cup, mix the wine with the serrano chile, garam masala, turmeric, cumin, and salt. Drizzle over the tofu while stirring the cubes.

Scatter the onion in the pot. Add the lentils and spread in an even layer. Blanket with the roasted chile.

Arrange the tofu in a layer in the pot. Top with layers of the cauliflower, zucchini, and tomatoes.

Cover and bake for about 30 minutes, or until 3 minutes after the aroma of a fully cooked meal escapes the oven. Serve immediately.

Israeli Tempeh

Tempeh is a soy-based product with a nubby texture. Tahini, or sesame paste, is commonly used in the Middle East as a dressing for falafel (fried chickpea patties) and is an ingredient in hummus and other dishes. Tahini separates when stored; be sure to mix it well before using. Both are easily found at natural food stores (look for tempeh in the refrigerated section next to the tofu).

I never peel beets for Glorious One-Pot Meals. Instead, I scrub them well with a brush and use a veggie wash to rinse away any residual grime. Then I simply slice them and toss them in the pot. Try golden beets in this recipe for a change from the typical red ones. They're just as sweet but won't color your entire meal red. SERVES 2

Olive oil spray

¹/₂ medium onion, sliced

One 8-ounce package tempeh (the 5-grain variety, if possible)

¹/₄ cup tahini

Juice of ¹/₂ lemon

3 to 5 garlic cloves, minced

2 tablespoons chopped fresh parsley

¹/₂ teaspoon Tabasco or other hot sauce

1 tablespoon balsamic vinegar

2 to 4 beets, preferably golden, thickly sliced

4 to 6 cremini mushrooms, thickly sliced

2 or 3 handfuls fresh spinach, chopped (2 or 3 loosely packed cups)

CALORIES 420 • PROTEIN 25G • CARBOHYDRATES 34G • FAT 26G • CHOLESTEROL 0 • SODIUM 128MG • FIBER 8G

Preheat the oven to 450°F.

Spray the inside and lid of a cast-iron Dutch oven with olive oil.

Scatter the onion in the pot. Lay the tempeh block on top of the onion.

In a small bowl, mix the tahini, lemon juice, garlic, parsley, Tabasco, and vinegar. Spoon half of the mixture over the tempeh.

Add a layer of beets and dollop with half of the remaining tahini mixture.

Arrange the mushrooms in a layer. Top with as much of the spinach as you can fit in the pot and still close the lid with a tight seal. Dollop the rest of the tahini mixture among the leaves.

Cover and bake for 35 minutes, or until 3 minutes after the aroma of a fully cooked meal escapes the oven. Serve immediately.

Pasta Primavera

Primavera *means "spring" in Italian. Pasta Primavera is a wonderfully colorful, light, and healthy meal filled with springtime vegetables. Almost any vegetable will go well in this dish. Consider adding English peas, sugar snap peas, spinach, asparagus, or other seasonal vegetables. Any type of squash or bell pepper is tasty as well. It doesn't matter whether your artichoke hearts are frozen or packed in water or oil, but remember that the oil from marinated artichokes will add a powerful punch. If you like heat, $^1/_4$ to $^1/_2$ teaspoon red pepper flakes can give this dish more of a kick.*

If there is still liquid in the bottom when the pot comes out of the oven, let it sit with the lid off for a few minutes, which will release some steam and allow the absorption of more of the liquid. Spoon any remaining liquid over each serving as a sauce. SERVES 2

Olive oil spray

2 cups multicolored or plain pasta (bow tie or ziti)

One 14-ounce can diced tomatoes

$^1/_2$ medium onion, chopped

3 to 5 garlic cloves, minced

$^1/_2$ teaspoon olive oil

8 to 10 ounces artichoke hearts, frozen, canned, or marinated, quartered

8 to 12 mushrooms, halved

1 medium zucchini, halved lengthwise and sliced

1 carrot, thinly sliced

$^1/_2$ teaspoon dried basil

$^1/_2$ teaspoon dried oregano

Sea salt and freshly ground black pepper

CALORIES 321 • PROTEIN 12G • CARBOHYDRATES 62G • FAT 2G • CHOLESTEROL 0 • SODIUM 655MG • FIBER 9G

Preheat the oven to 450°F.

Spray the inside and lid of a cast-iron Dutch oven with olive oil.

Spread the pasta in the bottom of the pot.

Drain the tomatoes, reserving $^2/_3$ cup liquid. (Add water if needed to make $^2/_3$ cup.) Add the onion, garlic, and the olive oil to the tomato liquid and pour it into the pot. Stir to coat the pasta evenly and make an even layer.

Add layers of the artichokes, mushrooms, zucchini, and carrot, periodically sprinkling with basil, oregano, salt, and pepper.

Pour the can of tomatoes over all and finish with a final sprinkle of spices.

Cover and bake for 45 minutes, or until 3 minutes after the aroma of a fully cooked meal escapes the oven. Serve immediately.

Lake Como Pasta

This easy pasta dish is fancy enough to serve to company, but simple enough for weekday dining. If you like spicy food, double the red pepper flakes (the amount given here is considered mildly to medium spicy). Or you can just leave them out. SERVES 2

Olive oil spray

2 cups radiatore, fusilli, or rotini

One 14-ounce can diced tomatoes

1 tablespoon chopped fresh basil

1 medium zucchini, halved lengthwise and thinly sliced

1 cup ricotta cheese

$^1/_4$ teaspoon red pepper flakes

$^1/_8$ teaspoon sea salt

$^1/_4$ teaspoon ground nutmeg

4 garlic cloves, chopped

$^1/_2$ cup sliced fresh porcini mushrooms, or $^1/_4$ cup dried (softened if necessary; see page 166)

Preheat the oven to 450°F.

Spray the inside and lid of a cast-iron Dutch oven with olive oil.

Arrange the pasta in the pot in an even layer.

Drain the tomatoes, reserving $^2/_3$ cup liquid. (Add water if needed to make $^2/_3$ cup.) Pour the liquid over the pasta and stir to coat the noodles.

Combine the basil in the can with the tomatoes and spread over the pasta. Add a layer of half of the zucchini.

In a small bowl, mix the ricotta with the red pepper flakes, salt, nutmeg, and garlic.

Spread the mixture over the zucchini, add the mushrooms, and top with the rest of the zucchini.

Cover and bake for 45 minutes, or until 3 minutes after the aroma of a fully cooked meal escapes the oven. Serve immediately.

CALORIES 489 • PROTEIN 24G • CARBOHYDRATES 58G • FAT 17G • CHOLESTEROL 50MG • SODIUM 734MG • FIBER 4G

Red Peppers, Mushrooms, and Barley

I love the depth of flavor offered from the blend of fresh and roasted red peppers here. These sweet notes play off the salty feta for a delicious contrast. SERVES 2

Olive oil spray

1/4 cup hulled or pearl barley

1/2 cup vegetable broth or water

1 cup feta cheese, crumbled

3 garlic cloves, minced

1/4 cup roasted red peppers packed in oil, sliced lengthwise

1 red bell pepper, cored, seeded, and cut into 1-inch slices

Juice of 1/2 lemon

2 portobello mushrooms, thickly sliced

2 cups roughly chopped greens (spinach, kale, etc.)

Preheat the oven to 450°F.

Spray the inside and lid of a cast-iron Dutch oven with olive oil.

Pour the barley and liquid into the pot. Stir to make an even layer. Scatter the feta and garlic in a layer.

Layer in the roasted and fresh red peppers and sprinkle with lemon juice. Arrange a thick layer of mushrooms and top with as many greens as you can fit in the pot and still close the lid with a tight seal.

Bake for 45 minutes, or until 3 minutes after the aroma of a fully cooked meal escapes the oven. Serve immediately.

VEGETARIAN
187

CALORIES 461 • PROTEIN 35G • CARBOHYDRATES 36G • FAT 25G • CHOLESTEROL 80MG • SODIUM 143MG • FIBER 6G

Sedona Peppers and Portobellos

This is a hearty vegetarian meal. The barley emerges al dente and a bit chewy, adding textural dimension to the meal and some of that meaty chewing satisfaction.

The more processed the barley, the softer it will be; that is, pearled barley will be softer than hulled barley. I prefer to use hulled barley as it is a whole grain; pearled barley is more refined.

SERVES 2

Olive oil spray
1/4 cup hulled barley
1/4 cup vegetable broth or water
1 red bell pepper, cored, seeded, and cut into 1-inch strips
1 green bell pepper, cored, seeded, and cut into 1-inch strips
4 ounces reduced-fat soft goat cheese (chevre), cut into 1/4-inch slices

3 to 5 garlic cloves, minced
One 4-ounce can chopped roasted green chiles
2 portobello mushrooms, thickly sliced
1/2 cup jarred roasted red peppers, cut into strips

Preheat the oven to 450°F.

Spray the inside and lid of a cast-iron Dutch oven with olive oil.

Pour the barley and liquid into the pot and stir to make an even layer.

Add a layer of the red and green bell peppers. Scatter half the cheese slices across the peppers. Sprinkle with the garlic and half of the green chiles.

Cut the mushroom slices into thirds and add to the pot. Top with the rest of the cheese, the roasted red peppers, and the rest of the green chiles.

Cover and bake for 50 minutes, or until 3 minutes after the aroma of a fully cooked meal escapes the oven. Serve immediately.

CALORIES 327 • PROTEIN 15G • CARBOHYDRATES 43G • FAT 13G • CHOLESTEROL 26MG • SODIUM 437MG • FIBER 6G

Turkish Eggplant

Believe it or not, eggplants have genders. Look for male eggplants, which have a shallow scar at their base, rather than female eggplants, which have a deeper indentation like a belly button. Male eggplants have fewer seeds and supposedly taste less bitter. SERVES 2

Olive oil spray
1/2 cup couscous
4 to 7 garlic cloves, minced or crushed
1/4 medium onion, chopped
1 small eggplant, peeled or not, cubed
Half of a 15-ounce can chickpeas, drained and rinsed
1/2 yellow or red bell pepper, cored, seeded, and cut into 1-inch squares
1 small zucchini, quartered lengthwise and cut into 1-inch slices

2 medium tomatoes, chopped, or one 15-ounce can diced tomatoes, drained
4 to 7 mushrooms, quartered
Sea salt and freshly ground black pepper
2 tablespoons chopped fresh marjoram, or 1 teaspoon dried
2 tablespoons chopped fresh parsley, or 1 teaspoon dried
2 tablespoons sesame seeds
2 teaspoons paprika
2 pinches red pepper flakes

Preheat the oven to 450°F.

Spray the inside and lid of a cast-iron Dutch oven with olive oil.

Pour the couscous and 1/2 cup water into the pot and stir to spread in an even layer. Scatter on half the garlic and onion.

Layer half the eggplant in the pot and top with half of the chickpeas, bell pepper, zucchini, tomatoes, and mushrooms. Sprinkle with salt and pepper and half of the marjoram, parsley, sesame seeds, paprika, and red pepper flakes. Repeat the layers, beginning with the eggplant.

Cover and bake for 40 minutes, or until 3 minutes after the aroma of a fully cooked meal escapes the oven. Serve immediately.

VEGETARIAN
189

CALORIES 361 • PROTEIN 14G • CARBOHYDRATES 70G • FAT 4G • CHOLESTEROL 0 • SODIUM 348MG • FIBER 15G

Sesame-Peanut Tofu

This is a great way to introduce kids to tofu. Be sure to press all the liquid out of the tofu before adding it to the pot so that it will absorb as much of the sesame and peanut flavors as possible. See page 168 for advice on pressing tofu.

I consider this recipe to be mildly spicy. If you need to make it blander for tender palates, use only $1/4$ teaspoon cayenne or none at all. If you like more heat, simply add more cayenne.

Instant brown rice has been parboiled, precooked, and then dried and packaged. It looks just like regular rice, except it is a whole grain rather than a refined one, and nothing artificial has been added. SERVES 2

2 teaspoons sesame oil

1 cup instant brown rice

$1^1/3$ cups vegetable broth

2 tablespoons peanut butter

2 tablespoons honey

2 tablespoons soy sauce

2 tablespoons rice wine vinegar

$1/8$ teaspoon ground ginger

2 to 4 garlic cloves, chopped

$1/2$ teaspoon cayenne

8 ounces firm tofu, drained, pressed, and cut into bite-size cubes

$1/2$ orange bell pepper, cored, seeded, and sliced

One 8-ounce can sliced water chestnuts, drained

$1/2$ head broccoli, cut into florets (about 2 cups)

CALORIES 807 • PROTEIN 35G • CARBOHYDRATES 122G • FAT 26G • CHOLESTEROL 0 • SODIUM 185MG • FIBER 11G

Preheat the oven to 450°F.

Wipe the inside and lid of a cast-iron Dutch oven with sesame oil.

Pour the rice and broth into the pot. Stir to coat the grains and smooth into an even layer.

In a medium bowl, whisk the peanut butter, honey, soy sauce, vinegar, ginger, garlic, and cayenne until the peanut butter is emulsified. Add the tofu and stir gently to coat the cubes. Add the tofu to the pot in an even layer, leaving some of the sauce in the bowl.

Scatter in the bell pepper, water chestnuts, and broccoli. Top with the rest of the peanut butter mixture.

Cover and bake for 50 minutes, or until 3 minutes after the aroma of a fully cooked meal escapes the oven. Serve immediately.

Sesame-Shiitake Tofu

I couldn't resist adding what is perhaps my favorite salad dressing to a Glorious One-Pot Meal. And, boy, was I glad I did, because besides the ease of using a prepared sauce, this was a vegetarian dinner that the whole family loved.

Frozen spinach works well in this recipe—just try to break the block into smaller chunks before adding to the pot. If the spinach has thawed, go ahead and squeeze out the water. If it is still frozen, don't worry about it.

Find arame seaweed at Asian markets or health food stores. SERVES 2

2 teaspoons sesame oil

$^1/_3$ cup dried arame seaweed, loosely packed

4 to 7 ounces extra-firm tofu, drained, pressed, and cut into cubes (see page 168)

3 tablespoons Annie's Sesame-Shiitake Vinaigrette (or other brand of sesame dressing)

1 cup sushi rice

8 to 10 shiitake mushrooms, roughly chopped

1 medium golden beet, cut into $^1/_4$-inch slices

2 cups chopped fresh spinach, or one 10-ounce package frozen

CALORIES 474 • PROTEIN 16G • CARBOHYDRATES 85G • FAT 8G • CHOLESTEROL 0 • SODIUM 145MG • FIBER 9G

Preheat the oven to 450°F.

Wipe the inside and lid of a cast-iron Dutch oven with sesame oil.

Place the arame in a small bowl and add enough water to cover. Set aside.

Put the tofu in a medium bowl with the vinaigrette. Stir gently to coat the cubes.

Rinse the rice in a strainer until the water runs clear, then add to the pot. Pour in 1 cup plus 1 tablespoon water and stir to make an even layer. Scatter the mushrooms in a layer. Cover with the beet slices. Top with the tofu, including any dressing in the bowl.

Strain and rinse the seaweed and scatter over the tofu. Finish with as much spinach as will fit in the pot.

Cover and bake for 45 minutes, or until 3 minutes after the aroma of a fully cooked meal escapes the oven. Serve immediately.

Sweet and Sour Tempeh

The Dutch discovered tempeh in Indonesia in the 1600s, but it has been used in Java for a thousand years. Tempeh is a fermented food made from partly cooked soybeans inoculated with spores of a friendly mold so that it transforms into a cheeselike product. It is firm with a slightly yeasty flavor until it soaks up whatever flavors you add, just as tofu does. Tempeh may be made with soybeans only or with soy and a grain such as rice, barley, or quinoa. Find it in the refrigerated section of the health food store, near the fresh tofu.

I'm not a fan of cilantro, but it is a traditional ingredient in some Asian cooking styles. Use it in this recipe or leave it out, whichever you prefer. SERVES 2

2 teaspoons sesame oil

1 cup white rice

Two 8-ounce packages tempeh, cut into bite-size cubes

1/4 cup teriyaki sauce

1 cup fresh or canned cubed pineapple

1/2 large sweet onion, sliced

1/2 yellow bell pepper, cored, seeded, and cut into strips

1/2 green bell pepper, cored, seeded, and cut into strips

1 cup cherry or grape tomatoes

2 tablespoons chopped fresh cilantro, optional

Preheat the oven to 450°F.

Coat the inside and lid of a cast-iron Dutch oven with sesame oil.

Rinse the rice in a strainer under cold water until the water runs clear. Pour the rice into the pot with 1 cup plus 2 tablespoons water. Stir to make an even layer.

Arrange the tempeh in a single layer on the rice. Drizzle with half of the teriyaki sauce. Scatter the pineapple, then the onion on top of the tempeh. Add the yellow and green bell pepper strips in a layer.

Place the tomatoes in any crevices and sprinkle with cilantro, if using.

Cover and bake for 45 minutes, or until 3 minutes after the aroma of a fully cooked meal escapes the oven. Serve immediately.

Sweet and Spicy Tofu

This recipe is 100 percent adaptable to whatever ingredients you have on hand. Try it with chicken pieces or strips, beef stew chunks, or turkey tenderloin (whole or in strips). I like to add some Brussels sprouts, yellow squash, any color bell pepper, or almost any vegetable found hiding in our fridge. After serving, be sure to scoop up all the sauce for maximum flavor.

The complex flavor of this marinade, with hints of sweet and spice, lends an Asian tang with a tinge of heat. Adjust the chili sauce to your desired level of hotness. You can also use chopped fresh or canned chiles or even a teaspoon of red pepper flakes. SERVES 2

2 teaspoons peanut oil

3 garlic cloves, minced or crushed

1 teaspoon grated fresh ginger

2 tablespoons fresh lime juice

1 teaspoon hoisin sauce

3 tablespoons soy sauce

$^1/_4$ cup white wine, sherry, or rice wine

1 teaspoon honey

$^1/_4$ teaspoon Asian chili sauce or chili oil

1 tablespoon chopped fresh parsley

1 tablespoon chopped fresh basil

6 to 8 ounces extra-firm tofu, drained, pressed, and cut into 1 x $^1/_2$-inch slices (see page 168)

1 cup sushi rice

2 carrots, sliced into coins

$^1/_4$ head cauliflower, cut into bite-size florets (about 2 cups)

$^1/_2$ red bell pepper, cored, seeded, and sliced

2 cups snow peas

Preheat the oven to 450°F.

Wipe the inside and lid of a cast-iron Dutch oven with peanut oil.

In a medium bowl, mix the garlic, ginger, lime juice, hoisin sauce, soy sauce, wine, honey, chili sauce, parsley, and basil.

Add the tofu cubes to the marinade. Stir to coat well and set aside.

Rinse the rice in a strainer under cold water until the water runs clear. Tip the rice into the pot, add 1 cup water, and stir to make an even layer. Add the carrots and cauliflower in a layer.

Layer the tofu in the pot, leaving some marinade in the bowl. Add the bell pepper and snow peas and pour the remaining marinade on top.

Cover and bake for 45 minutes, or until 3 minutes after the aroma of a fully cooked meal escapes the oven. Serve immediately.

Teriyaki Tempeh

Tempeh is a soy-based meat substitute. Find it in the refrigerated section, near the tofu, in health food stores. Not into tempeh? Try this with chicken, turkey, pork, shrimp, fish, or whatever you fancy!

In my opinion, low-sodium soy sauce tastes just as good as regular soy sauce. And feel free to substitute 3 tablespoons of a bottled teriyaki sauce for the soy/hoisin/peanut mixture.

Almost any vegetable tastes stupendous teriyaki-style. Try this recipe with broccoli, cauliflower, kale, bell peppers, zucchini, or any other vegetable you happen to have available. SERVES 2

Canola oil spray or 2 teaspoons peanut oil

1 cup sushi rice

One 8-ounce package tempeh, cut into $1/2$-inch strips

1 teaspoon Chinese 5-spice powder

1 tablespoon soy sauce

1 tablespoon hoisin sauce

1 tablespoon crushed peanuts (or peanut oil)

$1/4$ head red cabbage, shredded (about 2 cups)

2 carrots, sliced diagonally into thin ovals

5 to 10 mushrooms, thinly sliced

One 4-ounce can sliced water chestnuts, drained

CALORIES 594 • PROTEIN 37G • CARBOHYDRATES 110G • FAT 11G • CHOLESTEROL 0 • SODIUM 831MG • FIBER 7G

Preheat the oven to 450°F.

Spray the inside and lid of a cast-iron Dutch oven with canola oil or wipe with peanut oil.

Rinse the rice in a strainer under cold water until the water runs clear. Tip the rice into the pot, add 1 cup plus 1 tablespoon water, and stir to make an even layer.

Sprinkle the tempeh with the 5-spice powder and arrange on top of the rice.

In a small bowl, mix the soy sauce, hoisin sauce, and peanuts to make a teriyaki sauce. Spoon half the mixture over the tempeh.

Add the cabbage, carrots, mushrooms, and water chestnuts in layers. Pour the rest of the sauce over all.

Cover and bake for 45 minutes, or until 3 minutes after the aroma of a fully cooked meal escapes the oven. Serve immediately.

Thai Curry with Tofu

My cousin Julie learned this recipe when her sister, Abi, worked in Thailand. Julie throws in whatever vegetables she happens to have on hand, and the results are always outstanding. Instead of tofu, try substituting raw, peeled shrimp or scallops, chicken breasts, or fish fillets.

Notice that this recipe does not call for water to hydrate the rice. The coconut milk provides enough liquid to cook the rice and make a wonderful curry sauce. It doesn't seem to make any difference whether you use regular coconut milk or "lite."

Thai curry paste comes in yellow, red, and green—each works beautifully in this dish. Try the Mae Ploy brand found at Asian markets. Use more or less to taste; the amount here gives mild to medium heat. SERVES 2

Canola oil spray

1 cup jasmine rice

6 to 8 ounces extra-firm tofu, drained, pressed, and cubed (see page 168)

1/2 medium zucchini, quartered lengthwise and cut into 1-inch slices

One 4-ounce can bamboo shoots, drained and rinsed

1/2 red bell pepper, cored, seeded, and cut into 1-inch squares

1/2 yellow bell pepper, cored, seeded, and cut into 1-inch squares

One 14-ounce can coconut milk, regular or light

1 tablespoon Thai curry paste, red, green, or yellow

1 1/2 tablespoons fish sauce or soy sauce

2 teaspoons sugar

1/4 teaspoon paprika

1 tablespoon fresh lime juice

CALORIES 786 • PROTEIN 17G • CARBOHYDRATES 92G • FAT 41G • CHOLESTEROL 1MG • SODIUM 404MG • FIBER 7G

Preheat the oven to 450°F.

Spray the inside and lid of a cast-iron Dutch oven with canola oil.

Rinse the rice in a strainer under cold water until the water runs clear. Pour the rice into the pot and smooth into an even layer.

Arrange the tofu on top of the rice. Top with layers of the zucchini, bamboo shoots, and bell peppers.

In a medium bowl, whisk together the coconut milk, curry paste, fish sauce, sugar, paprika, and lime juice. (Be aware that coconut milk separates into liquid and solids when stored; be sure to use the entire contents of the can.) Whisk until the curry paste and sugar are dissolved. Pour the mixture evenly over the contents of the pot.

Cover and bake for 45 minutes, or until 3 minutes after the aroma of a fully cooked meal escapes the oven. Serve immediately.

Yemenite Lentils

This recipe has a Middle Eastern flair and is great as a vegetarian main course or a side dish for a larger meal. The lentils provide all the protein needed for a complete meal. Bulgur is a form of wheat (the wheat berries are steamed, dried, and ground) often used when making veggie burgers or tabbouleh. You can easily prepare this meal without the bulgur; just be sure to omit the water as well. SERVES 2

Olive oil spray

1/4 medium onion, sliced

1 cup bulgur

One 15-ounce can lentils, drained and rinsed

1/2 medium eggplant, cut into 1-inch cubes (about 2 cups)

4 to 6 garlic cloves, chopped

1 teaspoon ground cumin

1/2 teaspoon ground turmeric

1 teaspoon sea salt

1/2 teaspoon paprika

1/4 teaspoon cayenne

4 to 6 tomatoes, cut into wedges

2 cups chopped fresh spinach

Preheat the oven to 450°F.

Spray the inside and lid of a cast-iron Dutch oven with olive oil.

Scatter the onion in the pot.

In a medium bowl, combine the bulgur and $^1/_2$ cup water and pour into the pot in an even layer. Spoon the lentils on top of the bulgur.

Arrange half the eggplant in a layer.

In a small bowl, mix the garlic, cumin, turmeric, salt, paprika, and cayenne. Sprinkle about half of the spice mixture over the eggplant. Add the rest of the eggplant.

Fit the tomato wedges among the eggplant pieces and sprinkle with the rest of the spice mixture. Top with as much spinach as you can fit in and still retain a tight seal when you close the lid.

Cover and bake for about 45 minutes, or until 3 minutes after the aroma of a fully cooked meal escapes the oven. Serve immediately.

Zucchini Relleno

Modeled after the traditional cheese-stuffed, deep-fried green chiles that I adore so much at Mexican restaurants, this lighter, healthier version is almost as much fun to eat.

I like to use a mixture of mozzarella and Spanish Manchego cheeses, but you should use what you like. Often, I'll use soy cheese substitutes instead of real cheeses to make this a nondairy dinner that's lower in saturated fats and easier to digest. SERVES 2

Olive oil spray

2 scallions, white and green parts, chopped

1 medium zucchini, quartered lengthwise and cut into 1-inch slices

Sea salt

1 tablespoon chopped fresh cilantro, optional

1/2 medium yellow bell pepper, cored, seeded, and cut into 1/2-inch strips

4 to 8 ounces mozzarella or other cheese, grated

One 15-ounce can pinto beans, drained and rinsed

2 green chiles, stemmed, seeded, and chopped (try Anaheim or poblano)

2 medium tomatoes, chopped, or one 15-ounce can diced tomatoes, drained

2 or 3 fresh oregano sprigs

2 corn or whole wheat tortillas

CALORIES 500 • PROTEIN 30G • CARBOHYDRATES 66G • FAT 19G • CHOLESTEROL 50MG • SODIUM 153MG • FIBER 16G

Preheat the oven to 450°F.

Spray the inside and lid of a cast-iron Dutch oven with olive oil.

Scatter the scallions in the pot.

Spread the zucchini in a layer and season lightly with salt. Sprinkle with cilantro, if using.

Scatter in the bell pepper strips and top with half of the cheese. Cover with the pinto beans. Blanket with the green chiles.

Add the rest of the cheese and top with the tomatoes. Tuck the oregano sprigs in the crevices.

Spray each side of the tortillas with olive oil. Cut the tortillas in half and roll each half separately. Position the rolled tortilla halves on top of the other ingredients in the pot. Spray well with olive oil.

Cover and bake for about 35 minutes, or until 3 minutes after the aroma of a fully cooked meal escapes the oven. Serve immediately.

Green Chile Eggs

Although the edges will puff and brown appealingly, the center of this dish may remain moist because of the amount of green chile sauce used. Green chile sauce is not salsa (although salsa could easily be substituted here). I've been pleased to see more companies offering jarred or canned versions that seem to be making their way out of the Southwest and into the rest of the country. The amount of green chile sauce you use determines the heat level of your meal. Add another spice dimension with fresh or roasted green chiles, seeded and chopped.

Although this is a vegetarian recipe that calls for meat-substitute crumbles (find these in your grocer's freezer), you could easily add sausage, ground beef, pork, or turkey without changing anything else—likely not even the cooking time. Add chopped Canadian bacon and call it "green eggs and ham"! Consider whisking in $^1/_4$ cup milk with the eggs for a slightly more quichelike effect.

SERVES 2

Olive oil spray

1 medium sweet potato or yam, diced

$1^1/_2$ cups meat-substitute crumbles

$^2/_3$ cup mild green chile sauce, or to taste

$^1/_2$ red bell pepper, cored, seeded, and diced

$^1/_2$ green bell pepper, cored, seeded, and diced

3 to 5 mushrooms, sliced

$^1/_4$ head cauliflower, cut into bite-size florets (about 2 cups)

6 large eggs

$^1/_8$ teaspoon sea salt

CALORIES 442 • PROTEIN 39G • CARBOHYDRATES 36G • FAT 16G • CHOLESTEROL 639MG • SODIUM 734MG • FIBER 9G

Preheat the oven to 450°F.

Spray the inside and lid of a cast-iron Dutch oven with olive oil.

Spread the sweet potato in a thick layer. Cover with the meat substitute. Spoon $^1/_3$ cup of the green chile sauce on top.

Scatter the bell peppers and mushrooms into the pot. Add the cauliflower. Spread the rest of the chile sauce on top.

In a medium bowl, whisk the eggs with the salt. Pour the mixture evenly over all.

Cover and bake for about 35 minutes, or until 3 minutes after the aroma of a fully cooked meal escapes the oven. Serve immediately.

Eggs in a Nest

The eggs in this recipe emerge intact, similar to poached eggs. Hearty whole-grain bread or bread with sunflower or other seeds will add texture to this dish. SERVES 2

Olive oil spray

$^1/_2$ teaspoon cumin seeds or ground cumin

2 to 4 garlic cloves, thinly sliced

$^1/_2$ medium red onion, thinly sliced

$^1/_2$ orange bell pepper, cored, seeded, and thinly sliced

1 medium russet potato, cut into $^1/_2$-inch cubes

Sea salt and freshly ground black pepper

1 dried ancho or other chile, stemmed, seeded, and crushed

$^1/_2$ head Savoy cabbage, shredded or thinly sliced

4 large eggs

2 thick slices rustic bread, preferably whole grain and/or seeded

Preheat the oven to 450°F.

Spray the inside and lid of a cast-iron Dutch oven with olive oil.

Scatter the cumin seeds in the pot, followed by the garlic, onion, and bell pepper. Toss in the potato cubes and lightly season with salt and pepper. Sprinkle on the chile.

Pack in the cabbage. Make four wells in the cabbage, each large enough to hold an egg. Then crack each egg into a well, keeping the yolks intact. It's okay if the eggs leak out of their individual wells slightly. Lay the bread slices on top.

Cover and bake for 30 to 35 minutes, or until 3 minutes after the aroma of a fully cooked meal escapes the oven. Serve immediately.

CALORIES 420 • PROTEIN 23G • CARBOHYDRATES 57G • FAT 12G • CHOLESTEROL 426MG • SODIUM 462MG • FIBER 6G

INDEX

Aegean eggplant, 162–63
aloo gobi, 164–65
artichoke and mushroom pasta, 166–67
Boulder polenta, 168–69
curried veggies, 170–71
eggplant Parmesan, 172–73
eggplant with garlic sauce and sticky rice,
    174–75
eggs in a nest, 208
farmhouse pasta, 178
glorious macaroni and cheese, 176–77
Greek eggplant with bread stuffing, 179
green chile eggs, 206–7
Indian tofu, 180–81
Israeli tempeh, 182–83
Lake Como pasta, 186
pasta primavera, 184–85
red peppers, mushrooms, and barley, 187
Sedona peppers and portobellos, 188
sesame-peanut tofu, 190–91
sesame-shiitake tofu, 192–93
sweet and sour tempeh, 194–95
sweet and spicy tofu, 196–97
teriyaki tempeh, 198–99
Thai curry with tofu, 200–201
Turkish eggplant, 189
Yemenite lentils, 202–3
zucchini relleno, 204–5
Very, very mild fish, 58–59

Water chestnuts
    sesame-peanut tofu, 190–91
    teriyaki tempeh, 198–99

Yams. *See* Sweet potatoes
Yemenite lentils, 202–3
Yucatán fish, 60–61

Zucchini. *See also* Summer squash
    amaranth chili, 86–87
    chicken cacciatore, 122–23
    chicken Marsala, 126–27
    curried veggies, 170–71
    dill salmon, 28
    Far East fish, 29
    fish with herbes de Provence, 33
    flageolets and sausage, 96
    Greek chicken, 135
    honey-chili trout, 39
    Indian tofu, 180–81
    Lake Como pasta, 186
    pasta primavera, 184–85
    Scarborough Fair chicken, 149
    Thai curry with tofu, 200–201
    Turkish eggplant, 189
    zucchini relleno, 204–5

ABOUT THE AUTHOR

Elizabeth Yarnell is on a mission to help busy people eat healthy, home-cooked meals without sacrificing their time, money, or taste buds. After a 1999 diagnosis of multiple sclerosis forced her to take a good look at her diet and lifestyle, she dove into researching the connection between what we eat and how we feel. The infusion cooking technique she subsequently invented and patented has not only given her a way to manage the course of her health but also provided a quick and convenient weeknight dinner solution that satisfies the pickiest of eaters.

Now a Certified Nutritional Consultant (CNC) and Natural Health Professional (CNHP) as well as a cooking school instructor and healthstyle coach, Elizabeth enjoys sharing knowledge and ideas about healthy eating, natural health remedies, and living a natural lifestyle on her blog, Effortless Eating for Healthier Bodies (EffortlessEating.com).

Elizabeth's 2005 independently published cookbook, an earlier version of *Glorious One-Pot Meals,* spent eight weeks on the *Denver Post* bestseller list and was recognized by Best Books 2006; the National Indie Excellence Awards; iParenting Media, where it was named an Outstanding Product; and the Colorado Independent Publishers Association.

On her national tour Elizabeth speaks about healthy eating and cooking to audiences ranging from busy parents to empty nesters and from foodies looking for the next new cooking idea to MS patients and their patrons, heart disease sufferers, diabetics, cancer patients, and others who believe that bodies need and deserve good food. An event schedule can be found at GloriousOnePotMeals.com, along with answers to Glorious One-Pot Meal cooking questions, new recipes, video demonstrations, and much more.

Elizabeth lives in Denver, Colorado, with her husband and two children. The Glorious One-Pot Meal infusion cooking process holds U.S. (no. 6,846,504) and Canadian (no. 2,401,092) patents.